PRESENTED TO:

FROM:

DATE:

40 Days to Your Best Life

FOR MEN

HONOR HB BOOKS

Inspiration and Motivation for the Seasons of Life

COOK COMMUNICATIONS MINISTRIES
Colorado Springs, Colorado • Paris, Ontario
KINGSWAY COMMUNICATIONS LTD
Eastbourne, England

Honor® is an imprint of
Cook Communications Ministries, Colorado Springs, CO 80918
Cook Communications, Paris, Ontario
Kingsway Communications, Eastbourne, England

40 DAYS TO YOUR BEST LIFE FOR MEN
© 2006 by Honor Books

Manuscript written by Jay K. Payleitner
Interior Photo: © Kelly Pollak
Interior Design: Sandy Flewelling (TrueBlue Design)
Cover Design: BMB Design

First Printing, 2006
Printed in the United States of America

1 2 3 4 5 6 7 8 9 10 Printing/Year 11 10 09 08 07 06

ISBN 1-56292-707-8

To my dad and mom,
Ken and Marguerite Payleitner,
who taught me so much
and encouraged my quest.

Section 1 · RUNNING MAN

Day 1: Running Too Fast

Slow down, you move too fast.
You gotta make the morning last.
—Simon and Garfunkel

I'M GOING TO ASSUME this is the first devotional you've seen that begins with a quote from those great '60s theologians, Paul Simon and Art Garfunkel. But the sentiment they deliver in the first line of that classic tune is a reasonable admonition to most men in today's culture. We're moving so fast that we have already missed the morning, the afternoon is passing quickly, and we're burning daylight into the twilight of our lives.

Am I talking to you? Well, off the top of my head, here are a few questions that may help reveal your true pace.

- Do you barely complete all your work-related duties at the last second before (or just past) the assigned deadline?
- Do you regularly drive more than eight miles over the speed limit? (My cop friends tell me they usually don't issue tickets unless motorists pass that magical eight-over barrier.)
- Speaking of traffic, are you a weaver or can you sit patiently in the same lane for miles?
- Do you have more than three taped or TiVoed programs that you haven't found time to watch?
- When's the last time you held hands with a good woman and strolled through a park?
- When's the last time you read a good book?
- When's the last time you read the Good Book?
- Are you impatient with microwave ovens?
- In the middle of a heartfelt conversation with someone you care about, does your mind drift to deadlines, appointments, and stuff that needs to get done?

Admit it. You're moving so fast you don't even know what you're missing. And, frankly, it's not just kicking cobblestones and talking to lamp posts. You're oblivious to what the Creator of the universe has in mind for you.

But take heart because God will get your attention. Someday, somehow he is going to stop you in your tracks. He may use tragedy. He may send a message with a mentor. He may even use this little forty-day devotional.

So, men, stop running and stop battling the clock. The Bible even promises, "The LORD will fight for you; you need only to be still" (Ex. 14:14).

HEAVENLY FATHER, *we know that life on earth is nothing compared to the eternity of heaven. But that is beyond our comprehension, and so we allow ourselves to get caught up in the mock urgency and selfish business of today. Help us rest in you. Help us to stop running. Help us know you, our God. Amen.*

Better one handful with tranquillity than two handfuls with toil and chasing after the wind.
—Ecclesiastes 4:6

Day 2: Running the Wrong Way

Let us run with perseverance the race marked out for us.
—Hebrews 12:1

DESPITE WHAT WE SAID yesterday, running is not all bad. As a matter of fact, a footrace is used more than once in the Bible as a metaphor for our time here on earth. God promises to guide us on straight paths and "when you run, you will not stumble" (Prov. 4:11–12). He even promises a sweet reward for a well-run race: "Run in such a way as to get the prize" (1 Cor. 9:24).

So, upon further review, maybe the problem isn't that we're running too fast, it's that we're running in the wrong direction. We're lemmings running toward a finish line that is actually a thousand-foot cliff. We're racing up the corporate ladder only to discover it's leaning against the wrong building. We're looking for answers in the wrong book.

Don't mistake intensity and determination for success. In the 1929 Rose Bowl, Roy Riegels made a name for himself when he picked up a fumble, fought off a host of tacklers, and ran for sixty-five yards. Fortunately, one of his own teammates tackled him just before he crossed the wrong goal line.

So the question for today is this, "Which way are you headed?" An even more important question might be, "If you are headed the wrong way, do you have someone or something that will tackle you before you totally mess things up?" I hope you do. As men, we are compelled to explore and take risks. But if we don't have a compass (or a friend with a compass) we're going to lose our way.

This forty-day devotional is going to show you that stopping and asking for directions is not all bad. Look again at that great verse at the top of this chapter. At first glance the challenge is to "run with perseverance." But for many guys that's not the problem—we would eagerly dedicate our lives to something worthwhile and run with great determination. It's the second half of the equation that trips us up. Many of us are too busy running to see the road signs that God has clearly placed at each and every intersection. So, men, wipe the sweat from your eyes and set your sights on "the race marked out for us."

HEAVENLY FATHER, *we are so eager to know your plan for our lives. We want to serve you and enjoy all your blessings. But we confess that when we get lost, the first thing we do is try to find our own way. Instead, Lord, help us find your way. Help us run the course you want us to run with supernatural perseverance. Amen.*

**It is not good to have zeal without knowledge,
nor to be hasty and miss the way.**
—Proverbs 19:2

Day 3: Running on Empty

May the force be with you.
—Obi-Wan Kenobi

LET'S BE CLEAR. "The force" is nothing more than a multibillion-dollar empire that made George Lucas famous and rich. Beyond the pages of a screenplay, it's a myth. Still, as guys, we're fascinated by any source that promises to provide power beyond our own ability, whether that's "the force" or "the matrix" or whatever.

Sure, we like to present ourselves as self-sufficient. We refuse to stop for directions. We put off going to the doctor. Our first attempts at assembling anything are done without looking at the instructions. We value rugged individualism and independence. But in the middle of the night as we stare up at the ceiling in the dark, we confess that we can't make it on our own. Although we may not readily admit it, our most desperate need is to plug into a power that's beyond ourselves. When push comes to shove—on our own—we're running on empty.

Our quest for power takes some of us to the weight room, health food store, or local steroid provider. Others seek power in conference rooms and advanced education. Some men sadly wield the dark side of power through physical, emotional, verbal, and sexual abuse. Ultimately, every one of these power-grabbers comes up empty.

So how do we satisfy our power fix? Paradoxically, gaining power often takes an act of surrender. It turns out the Creator of the universe has power to spare. And he wants to share it with you. All you have to do is acknowledge his lordship, ask, and believe. As a matter of fact, if you're on his team, he's actively looking to fill your tank. In the Bible we read, "For the eyes of the LORD range throughout the earth to strengthen those whose hearts are fully committed to him" (2 Chron. 16:9).

So what's your power source? May his force be with you.

HEAVENLY FATHER, *You are the Alpha and the Omega, the beginning and the end. You are all-knowing and all-powerful. You put the stars in place. You know our every need. We would be fools to look anywhere else for power. Lord, open our eyes to who you are and help us be dependent on you and you alone. Amen.*

I tell you the truth, if you have faith as small as a mustard seed, you can say to this mountain, "Move from here to there" and it will move. Nothing will be impossible for you.
—Matthew 17:20

Day 4: Go or No Go?

It ain't those parts of the Bible that I can't understand
that bother me, it is the parts that I do understand.
—Mark Twain

BACK WHEN I WAS in my midtwenties, I spent two
years of my life lugging a twenty-three-pound briefcase
around downtown Chicago and Milwaukee trying to sell
law books to corporate attorneys. If you were a client, I
apologize. I had no idea what I was talking about. But I'll
never forget the day my sales manager was traveling with
me and he expressed an urgency for me to close a couple
big sales before the month ended. He said, "Don't you get
it? You're on 'go or no go.'" Well, I finally did get the message, and I eked out a few more months with that company

before leaving the commission sales game for good. Hey, when you're on "go or no go," it's a good idea to leave before they fire you.

And now you need to answer the same question. Will you go? Or no go? Are you truly ready to commit to seeking God's best? Do you really want to know what the Bible says? This next section of the devotional (and don't say I didn't warn you) covers some ground that may make you a little uncomfortable at first.

This is day four in our forty-day journey, and it really hasn't been too painful, but that's about to change. So this is where you either commit to going all the way or unceremoniously slide this book onto a dusty bookshelf alongside all the other shoulda/coulda reading rejects.

Let me lay it out for you. Over the next ten days, we're going to be taking a hard look at some of the garbage in your life. Stuff you may not want to think about. God's light may illuminate some dark corners that you thought were pretty well hidden and mostly harmless. Now peeking into those corners may sound a little risky, but don't worry, it's all part of the process. The Bible says, "Whenever anyone turns to the Lord, the veil is taken away" (2 Cor. 3:16).

Then around day fifteen, we're going to turn the corner

and open up a box of tools that will help tear down the old you and start building up a new you. After all, we promised you "forty days to your best life."

But here's where we confess that the title of this book is a bit deceiving. You see, before we're through, the goal is really for you to surrender your life all the way over to God. So truthfully, we're not headed toward "your best life." The actual goal is "God's best life for you." See you tomorrow.

HEAVENLY FATHER, *I have been keeping you at arm's length for far too long. I've been running too fast, running the wrong way, and running under my own power. But, with your help, I'm ready to change all that. I want to live my life for you and with you. I know I've got some work to do, but I'm not afraid. Amen.*

**Search me, O God, and know my heart;
test me and know my anxious thoughts.
See if there is any offensive way in me,
and lead me in the way everlasting.**
—Psalm 139:23–24

Section 2 · FULL DISCLOSURE

Day 5: Like Father, Like Son

If you build it, he will come.
—The whisper in Ray Kinsella's cornfield
Field of Dreams

AS PROMISED, WE'RE GOING to start digging into who you are so you can figure out how to proceed. That exercise begins with you as a boy.

Now that last phrase—"you as a boy"—very likely released a flood of emotions, which confirms that your formative years are indeed a good place to start digging. The truth is that there may be some junk you need to deal with from your past—especially between you and your father. A Gallup poll commissioned by the highly respected National Center for Fathering found that 56 percent of men agreed with the statement, "Most people have unresolved problems with their fathers." That may or may not surprise you.

Author Gordon Dalbey uses the descriptive term "father wound" in his books. Dr. Ken Canfield, author and president of the National Center for Fathering, uses the phrase "fathering deficit" and challenges any man who was never well connected to his own father to work at becoming an "overcomer dad." Canfield even suggests that all men do some soul searching and seriously assess the ways that we are similar to and different from our fathers. You may want to take out a sheet of paper and list the ways you and your father are alike and not alike when it comes to habits, temperament, communication style, addictions, discipline techniques, etc.

After your exercise, you may want to have a heart-to-heart with your dad. Not to stir up anger or lay blame, but to help put the past in perspective, ask for and give forgiveness, and merely catch up on who both of you are today. You can expect some raw emotion and tears, and some of you may even experience a brick wall. For those of you whose fathers have passed away or who don't have any way to contact your fathers, the exercise is still valid if you approach it honestly and work to see both sides of the relationship.

For you fortunate guys who enjoyed and still have a great relationship with your father, count your blessings and work to keep that legacy going. Out of your overflow of fathering connectiveness, you may find great satisfaction in identifying fatherless boys in your community and pouring yourself into their lives. But most men, I suspect, can identify with Ray Kinsella who plowed under his cornfield and built a ball field just so he could play catch with his father. What are you willing to do to reconnect with yours?

HEAVENLY FATHER, *we are humbled that you want us to be part of your family. We are stunned that Jesus is our brother and we are heirs of your kingdom. Forgive us our transgressions and help us forgive those who have hurt us. Unite our families within your family. Help us be the kind of sons and fathers you want us to be. Amen.*

**Honor your father and your mother,
so that you may live long in the land
the LORD your God is giving you.**
—Exodus 20:12

Day 6: The Root of All Kinds of Evil

I've got all the money I'll ever need,
just so long as I die by four o'clock.
—Henny Youngman

HAVE YOU EVER MET someone who pompously stated that the Bible is out of date and has no application to today's world? Well, all you have to do is point him to what Scripture has to say on the topic of money. It's surprising, honest, penetrating, and universally relevant. Guys in every tax bracket have firsthand experience about how money can absolutely control your life.

The Bible has some five hundred verses concerning faith and about five hundred on the topic of prayer, but more than twenty-three hundred on money and possessions. Here are just a few that speak right to the heart of men:

Whoever loves money never has money enough; who-ever loves wealth is never satisfied with his income. (Eccl. 5:10)

No one can serve two masters. Either he will hate the one and love the other, or he will be devoted to the one and despise the other. You cannot serve both God and Money. (Matt. 6:24)

For the love of money is a root of all kinds of evil. Some people, eager for money, have wandered from the faith and pierced themselves with many griefs. (1 Tim. 6:10)

For where your treasure is, there your heart will be also. (Luke 12:34)

The funny thing is that the Bible never says money itself is bad. The love of money is bad. Greed is bad. Seeing a brother in need and not sharing is bad. Attempting to get rich quick leads to destruction. But the truth is that money and possessions are not inherently evil. David, Solomon, Job, Abraham, and other biblical heroes were abundantly wealthy, but for the most part they had their act together when it came to money.

So how can you get your act together about money so that it doesn't control you? To stop the stranglehold money has on us, we need to recognize the temporal nature of possessions. Earthly stuff doesn't last. Besides, all the riches of the world were created by and are still owned by God. Our houses, our cars, our clothes, and our computers are merely on loan from a generous provider. In return, our job is to be grateful and keep praying, "Give us this day our daily bread." And, you know what? He will.

HEAVENLY FATHER, *I know I will never be able to serve you with my whole heart until I stop chasing after material possessions. Help me to loosen my grip on my finances. Help me to be content with all the riches you have already given me. Open my eyes and soften my heart to those in need. Amen.*

Do not store up for yourselves treasures on earth, where moth and rust destroy, and where thieves break in and steal. But store up for yourselves treasures in heaven, where moth and rust do not destroy, and where thieves do not break in and steal.

—Matthew 6:19–20

Day 7: Only Dogs Get Mad, Right?

A quick-tempered man does foolish things.
—Proverbs 14:17

IN THE FURY OF the moment, why does it feel so satisfying to rage in anger? Then, when the rant ends, why do we feel so cruddy?

It doesn't matter whether the rage is unspoken seething or out loud bellowing. Men seem to like to stomp, snort, gnash their teeth, and lash out at anyone standing within earshot. The trouble is that those who are close to us are, indeed, close to us. We tend to hurt those we love.

After any outburst, of course, we feel demoralized and try to explain it away or cover it up with a meaningless, half-hearted apology, which makes the whole episode even worse. Face it, men can be real jerks. And believe me, it takes one to know one.

One of the great ironies about anger is that, while we allow ourselves to enter that uncontrollable state because we feel we have been wronged, perhaps the event that led to our outburst is actually part of God's best plan for our lives. We get angry when a girl rejects our request for a date, but she wasn't our soul mate anyway. We get angry when our son doesn't make the basketball team, but that leads to new opportunities in some other activity. We get angry when we don't get a promotion, but a better career path is just around the corner.

There's a story of a man shipwrecked for months on a desert island. When his primitive, handmade hut is destroyed by lightning, he shakes his fist at heaven. Hours later he is stunned when the captain of a ship tells him, "We came because we saw your smoke signals."

When anger goes unchecked, it's not unusual to embarrass ourselves by fuming about stuff that is unrelated to our anger. We get mad at traffic jams, vending machines, cell phones, umpires, food servers, and customer service agents. In the end, we come off looking foolish. Proverbs says, "A patient man has great understanding, but a quick-tempered man displays folly" (Prov. 14:29).

The apostle Paul says, "In your anger do not sin" (Eph. 4:26). That's an excellent warning. But it also suggests that there is a kind of anger that is not sinful. Jesus modeled righteous anger in John 2 when he overturned the tables of the moneychangers who had desecrated his father's house, turning it into a "den of thieves." Just so, we should be angry when faced with issues like child abuse, racism, abortion, and other injustices. Anger can be a force for good.

How can we make sure we limit our anger to the righteous kind? We need to ask, "What would make God angry?"

In James we read, "Take note of this: Everyone should be quick to listen, slow to speak and slow to become angry, for man's anger does not bring about the righteous life that God desires" (1:19–20).

HEAVENLY FATHER, *help us to listen, exhibit self-control, and really consider the big picture when things don't seem to go our way. Help us be slow to anger and quick to sincerely ask forgiveness when we fail to hold our tongues. Lord, when we are angry with you, we ask for your mercy—mercy we do not deserve. Amen.*

**"In your anger do not sin": Do not let the
sun go down while you are still angry.**
—Ephesians 4:26

Day 8: Word Up

Sticks and stones may break my bones,
but words can never hurt me.
—Highly inaccurate playground platitude

BESIDES ANGRY OUTBURSTS, there are all kinds of ways that a man's words can stir up trouble. Conventional wisdom suggests men may not gossip like women, but we have our own damaging ways of using words. Most of our foot-in-mouth experiences come out of our tendency to indiscreetly say whatever comes to mind. Like the T-shirt says, "Engage brain before opening mouth."

The consequences of not holding your tongue can be severe. You can lose your job for lying or harassing. Sarcasm and bragging will keep your friends at a distance. Words that belittle, accuse, or criticize will damage your marriage. Jokes about your young daughter's eating habits may lead to a serious case of anorexia during her teenage years. You can build your son up or tear him down with a mere handful of words.

I will never forget a brief conversation I had with my dad during my junior year of high school after taking first place in a junior varsity wrestling tournament. The trophy was small, but I had fought hard to earn it. He held it in his hand and said, "Maybe next year you can win a varsity trophy." Now, of course, he meant it as a challenge to keep working hard and reach for the stars. But at that moment, his words cut me like a knife. The Bible has a great teaching for men—especially dads—on this matter. "Rejoice with those who rejoice; mourn with those who mourn" (Rom. 12:15). When anyone comes to you with emotional news, your best response is to reflect his or her demeanor right back to them. In the moment, celebrate in their joy or join them in their sorrow. Use phrases like, "That's fantastic" or "Oh, man, I'm so sorry." There's plenty of time for advice, correction, planning, or personal challenges a little later on. Whenever possible, laugh or cry right along with the people you care about most.

So let's watch our words. The Bible cautions that "out of the same mouth come praise and cursing" (James 3:10). But the answer is not to sit silently in fear of saying something we may later regret. Instead, we need to practice the art of picking and polishing our words a little more carefully. Proverbs tells us "a word aptly spoken is like apples of gold" (25:11).

HEAVENLY FATHER, *let my heart reflect your heart. Let my words reflect your love. Let my voice, my mind, my heart, and my hands give praise to you our Creator. Help me be an encourager and loving witness for you. Give me the right words at the right time in all matters. And help me know when to hold my tongue. Amen.*

Whoever would love life and see good days
must keep his tongue from evil
and his lips from deceitful speech.
—1 Peter 3:10

Day 9: No Fear

Do not be anxious about anything, but in everything, by prayer
and petition, with thanksgiving, present your requests to God.
And the peace of God, which transcends all understanding,
will guard your hearts and your minds in Christ Jesus.
—Philippians 4:6–7

WHAT ARE YOU AFRAID OF? Is it spiders? Did you know that arachnophobia is the most common phobia in western culture? Half of all women and 10 percent of men have a fear of the eight-legged creepy crawlies. Below is a list of the ten most common phobias.

1. Arachnophobia—Fear of spiders
2. Anthrophobia—Fear of people, especially speaking in public

3. Aerophobia—Fear of flying
4. Agoraphobia—Fear of open spaces
5. Claustrophobia—Fear of confined spaces
6. Acrophobia—Fear of heights
7. Emetophobia—Fear of vomit
8. Carcinophobia—Fear of cancer
9. Brontophobia—Fear of thunderstorms
10. Necrophobia—Fear of death or dead things

Do you suffer from any of these phobias in such a way that your life is handicapped? If not, what are you afraid of? (I'm amazed snakes aren't on the list.) Maybe your fears run much deeper—like the fear of missing your purpose in life or fear of failure.

Honestly, the only thing we really need to fear is God.

Not to be confusing, but the fear of God is different than the ten phobias listed above. It's more about approaching God with absolute awe, respect, and reverence. What's more, once we accept God's love, we never have to be afraid again. The Bible teaches, "There is no fear in love. But perfect love drives out fear" (1 John 4:18).

A story about Craig Reynolds, two-time All-Star shortstop for the Houston Astros, makes the point in a practical human way. A reporter asked Reynolds, "Suppose it's the bottom of the ninth inning and your team is down by one run. You're at the plate with the bases loaded, two outs, and a three-two count. The next pitch will decide the game. If you get a hit, two runs score and you're the hero. If you strike out, you're the goat. With fifty-six thousand fans yelling at the top of their lungs, how do you deal with that sort of pressure? How do you handle your performance fears?" Reynolds replied, "I know that when the game is over, I'm going to drive home to a family and to a church who are going to love me no matter what. Whether I get a hit or strikeout won't alter how they feel about me. Knowing they are going to love me—no matter what I do—allows me to step up to the plate, relax, and do the best that I can."

Perfect, unconditional love—which only God can give—can free us to be our best. From an eternal perspective, we never have to be afraid of anything ever again. Not death. Not insignificance. Not Satan. Not even snakes.

HEAVENLY FATHER, *we stand in awe of who you are and how much you love us. We know you are in control of every situation and every challenge we face. We trust that you will protect us and provide our every need. We are not afraid. Amen.*

The LORD himself goes before you and will be with you; he will never leave you nor forsake you. Do not be afraid; do not be discouraged.
—Deuteronomy 31:8

Day 10: Lonely Miles

Loneliness and the feeling of being unwanted
is the most terrible poverty.
—Mother Teresa

HAVE YOU EVER FELT alone in a crowded room? Have you ever wondered if your friends were really your friends? Have you ever thought, *No one knows me. No one really cares. No one would miss me if I wasn't here. I might as well be invisible?*

Before you lose yourself in a deep funk, please know that most of us have been there. We enter an empty room and turn on the TV for company. We ride a crowded elevator among strangers. On a street corner, faceless crowds scurry past and we stand still among the blur of activity.

If all this leaves you feeling lost in the cold, there are two things you need to consider.

First, you're not alone. The last words in the gospel of Matthew are Jesus' promise to his followers: "And surely I am with you always, to the very end of the age" (Matt. 28:20). That's always worth remembering, especially during those times when our human friends have ditched us.

Second, maybe you're getting loneliness confused with solitude. You know, solitude can be a powerful force for good. The Bible tells us that even Jesus would often slip away to the wilderness for some time alone. "But Jesus often withdrew to lonely places and prayed" (Luke 5:16).

If Jesus—who was fully God—needed to get away for some quiet meditation, doesn't it make sense that we should as well? That could mean forty days of prayer and fasting, or it could mean brief moments stolen from everyday life. One of my favorite poems from Robert Frost creates a compelling image of a man who paused for a moment to assess his life and recommit to his mission and his promise.

Stopping by Woods on a Snowy Evening

Whose woods these are I think I know.
His house is in the village, though;

He will not see me stopping here
To watch his woods fill up with snow.

My little horse must think it queer
To stop without a farmhouse near
Between the woods and frozen lake
The darkest evening of the year.

He gives his harness bells a shake
To ask if there is some mistake.
The only other sound's the sweep
Of easy wind and downy flake.

The woods are lovely, dark, and deep,
But I have promises to keep,
And miles to go before I sleep,
And miles to go before I sleep.

I'm a little envious of this man, aren't you? Clearly, the sleigh driver has a destination and a schedule, but still he finds time to pause and appreciate the moment. Of course, you can dig pretty deep into these sixteen lines and question whether "woods" and "sleep" may be metaphors for "life" and "death." But the point is that when you find yourself alone—or lonely—God might be calling you to heed the words of Psalm 46:10, "Be still, and know that I am God."

HEAVENLY FATHER, *thank you for being a friend and a refuge when I am feeling lost and alone. Thank you for caring about every aspect of my life. Thank you for continually calling my name and drawing me to yourself. Thank you for being there through the storms and in the quiet. Amen.*

Come near to God and he will come near to you.
—James 4:8

Day II: The Pecking Order

All we are is dust in the wind.
—Kansas, "Dust in the Wind"

LET'S SEE NOW. That guy over there is a CEO, so obviously he's worth more than me. That other guy is on the school board, so he also has me beat. My car is faster than the guy down the street, but his house is bigger than mine. My girlfriend is prettier. His kid made all-conference. We guys love to compete, don't we?

When we walk into a dinner party or business meeting, we instantly compare ourselves to the rest of the group. We rank ourselves by our cars, houses, incomes, and job titles. We also do a bit of judging in the locker room showers, but we won't go there.

A lot of guys think they're pretty darn special and need a dose of humility. Other guys are getting beat up by the world, feeling like crud, and could use a shot of self-esteem. So how do we put a price tag on ourselves?

Scientists tell us we are 98 percent water and the rest of the elements in our physical bodies are worth less than a buck. Genesis tells us "for dust you are and to dust you will return" (Gen. 3:19). For many guys, their paycheck each week tells them exactly what they're worth.

But the best way to determine the value of an item is by identifying something for which it can be exchanged. A cup of coffee at Starbucks costs about what you'd pay for a new baseball. The cost of a sunroom addition is about what you'd pay for a Lexus.

Gentlemen, hold on to your hats because you may not have thought about this before. But here's the greatest truth you'll ever hear: You are worth Jesus.

He traded his life for yours. Theologians sometimes even call Jesus' substitutionary death "the great exchange." As a matter of fact, if you were the only person who ever lived, he would have died on the cross to pay the penalty for your sins.

While that sinks in, take a moment to gain control

over your pride and egocentric ways with this pledge: "I will stop boasting. I will stop beating up on myself. I will stop comparing myself to others. After all, Jesus gave his life for me."

Now that is a truth worth boasting about, and the Bible says go for it. Paul wrote, "May I never boast except in the cross of our Lord Jesus Christ, through which the world has been crucified to me, and I to the world" (Gal. 6:14).

HEAVENLY FATHER, *it's so clear that the only way my life can have any true value is through my relationship with you. It doesn't matter how I compare to others because no matter what, my sins cause me to fall far, far short of your glory. Compared to you, I am dust. But with you, I can accomplish great things.*

For whoever exalts himself will be humbled, and whoever humbles himself will be exalted.

—Matthew 23:12

Day 12: The Most Difficult Chapter

Flee from sexual immorality.
— 1 Corinthians 6:18

THERE'S NOT A LOT of gray area on this matter. Men, throw away your porn. All of it.

Throw away any magazines with naked or scantily clad women, including all those *Sports Illustrated* swimsuit editions and Victoria's Secret catalogs. Throw away every DVD or video with an R rating or worse, unless it truly has some redeeming value. Shut down your computer until you can install a porn filter and/or pledge that you will never, ever visit another questionable site or respond to a questionable e-mail solicitation. Purpose in your heart today that you will never again walk into a Hooters restaurant or any other establishment that is in the business of marketing and displaying women as sex objects.

In every one of these areas—magazines, videos, Web surfing, entertainment—draw a line in the sand and do not cross it.

By the way, making these changes is impossible—if you expect to do it under your own power. Men are wired and conditioned to pursue graphic sexual images and, honestly, we are helpless without turning it over to our Creator. We need to ask God for courage and strength. We need to ask God to shield our eyes even as we take that garbage to the trash can. We need to ask God to help us "bounce our eyes," instantly looking away from women with tight or revealing outfits, a technique described in Stephen Arterburn's best seller *Every Man's Battle*. We need to hold each other accountable to "flee from sexual immortality."

Why? Submitting to the power of pornography prevents you from enjoying healthy relationships with women. It robs your time and attention, keeping you from fulfilling God's plan for your life. It erases your testimony. It finances a trillion-dollar industry that should sicken your stomach. Maybe worst of all, it robs you of a chance to fully devote yourself to God.

Need more persuading? Imagine dying tomorrow. Then picture your loved ones finding that stash of pornography under your bed or in the back of your cabinet. Imagine your wife, boss, mother, son, or daughter reviewing your credit card bills or checking the log of your recent Web activity. Imagine Jesus hanging out with you for the past week.

Gentlemen—for your family, for your future, for your soul—throw out your porn.

HEAVENLY FATHER, *I choose today to destroy these images that do so much damage. I purpose in my heart to flee from even a hint of sexual immorality. But I cannot do this alone. Lead the way, Lord. Lead the way to a pure heart and a pure mind so that I can serve you in all things at all times. And help me model this new freedom to other men. Amen.*

**But among you there must not be
even a hint of sexual immorality.**
—Ephesians 5:3

Day 13: Do Your Own Thing

This above all: to thine own self be true.
—Polonius's advice to his son, Laertes, in
William Shakespeare's Hamlet *(1.3)*

NO. NO. NO. Just because Shakespeare said it, doesn't make it true. Just because "being true to yourself" is the prevailing mantra of our culture doesn't mean it's the right choice. As a matter of fact, God's way is quite often just the opposite of our natural instincts as humans. Hey, remember the garden of Eden? Left to our own devices, we make bad choices. Add that hissing Satan scoundrel to cloud our decision making even further, and we end up naked and homeless.

The '60s told America, "If it feels good, do it." Today's version says the same thing, but with a darker, in-your-face tone: "Who's to say what's right or wrong? Don't you dare impose your values on me." If that sounds reasonable to you, consider this story from my own experience.

A few years ago, I was hired to develop content for a Web site designed for teenagers to log on and find answers to life's toughest problems. The big, government-grant-sponsored project kept me on the job for only a few weeks because I kept trying to interject biblical truths and absolutes into the Web links. Silly me, I thought kids should be guided toward moral choices. Well, it turns out the secular Web site sponsors didn't want kids to have to worry about ridiculous notions such as right and wrong, and most of my content was "revised." Ultimately, in case after case—when faced with issues such as cheating, lying, sexual experimentation, parental authority, etc., the best advice this popular Web site currently has to offer is "search your heart and just do what you think is best."

Yikes! I don't think we want to live in a world in which teenagers are left to follow their own whims and desires. Teens need guidance beyond their experiences. We men also need guidance beyond our experiences. Admit it. Left to our own best instincts, we stink.

Conversely, true wisdom and empowerment come

when you turn to the Creator of the universe and say, "Help." As a matter of fact, if you're on his team, he's looking to fill your tank. "For the eyes of the LORD range throughout the earth to strengthen those whose hearts are fully committed to him" (2 Chron. 16:9).

HEAVENLY FATHER, *we freely admit that you are the source of all power and wisdom. But somehow we still think we can make it on our own. Lord, please take those egotistical thoughts from our heads, and fill us with your grace, your truth, and your power. Amen.*

**For the wisdom of this world
is foolishness in God's sight.**
—1 Corinthians 3:19

Day 14: You've Got a Problem and It Has a Name

*I do not understand what I do. For what I want to do
I do not do, but what I hate I do.*
—Romans 7:15

WANTING TO LAY A foundation of prayer for an upcoming outreach event, a traveling evangelist wrote a letter to the mayor of the city asking for the names of individuals who were spiritually in crisis. The mayor surprised the preacher by sending him a city phone book.

The evangelist shouldn't have been surprised. And neither should we. It's been quite clear since the garden of Eden that all men are born with a terminal condition known as sin. Anyone who denies our inclination to make unwise choices and put ourselves first is kidding himself. Observe human nature and you'll see infinite examples of our fallen nature. Watch a toddler react when another youngster takes his favorite toy. Watch a group of men react when a well-proportioned woman in a revealing outfit enters the room. Listen to the life stories of addicts, compulsive gamblers, and prostitutes. Talk to neighbors and coworkers. Talk to authentic Christians. Search your own heart. Don't deny it—we are living proof of the words in Romans: "for all have sinned and fall short of the glory of God" (Rom. 3:23).

The last several devotions have touched on a variety of sinful and paralyzing conditions common to man: greed, anger, fear, sarcasm, lying, pride, lust, and self-reliance. You can create your own list that applies to guys you know: sloth, hate, envy, racism, stealing, boastfulness, etc. But before you start pointing fingers, take an inventory of your own life. That's what Jesus was talking about when he said, "Why do you look at the speck of sawdust in your brother's eye and pay no attention to the plank in your own eye?" (Luke 6:41).

Too many of us refuse to acknowledge the sin in our lives, even though we take a perverse delight in judging others. That's a particularly precarious situation. Listen to the warning Paul wrote to the members of the church at Corinth.

So, if you think you are standing firm, be careful that you don't fall! No temptation has seized you except what is common to man. And God is faithful; he will not let you be tempted beyond what you can bear. But when you are tempted, he will also provide a way out so that you can stand up under it. (1 Cor. 10:12–13)

Once again, God knows what's going on in our heads and has already provided for all our needs. He knows our temptations. He knows our weaknesses. But he also has given us a way out! He has  even given us a whole arsenal of weapons with which to combat our sinful conditions. That's what the next section is all about: arming yourself for battle.

A wise man once said, "The first step to solving any problem is identifying the problem." Well, the problem is sin and it's persistent and pervasive. So, attention sinners: Get ready for Section 3.

HEAVENLY FATHER, *as difficult as it is, thank you for opening my eyes to the sin in my life. Help me fully understand how it breaks your heart and keeps me from drawing closer to you. When we consider the sin in our lives, we finally understand that we need you more than ever. Amen.*

When you bow down before the Lord and admit your dependence on him, he will lift you up.
—James 4:10 NLT

Section 3: YOUR SPIRITUAL TOOLBOX

Day 15: First … Worship

Our God is an awesome God. He reigns
from heaven and earth, with wisdom, power,
and love. Our God is an awesome God.
—Rich Mullins, "Awesome God"

AFTER YEARS OF BUILDING a reputation as a mischief maker, a young lad suddenly becomes the teacher's pet at Sunday school. When she asks a question of the class, he's the first to raise his hand and always has something wise to contribute. His buddy in the class knows he's pulling a fast one and gets him to reveal his secret. "It's easy," says the boy. "Every time Mrs. Gundersen asks a question, I just say, 'I think we should pray more and read the Bible.' That's the right answer for everything."

The boy is right. Everything we need to know about God and his plan for us is in the Bible. And every prayer we pray is heard and answered. (And we'll cover both of those tools over the next couple days.) But to get to the point where our heart is ready to communicate with God and understand God's Word, I believe it's imperative to first bring our hearts and minds to a place of authentic worship.

Worship is recognizing God as Creator, King, Father, and Redeemer and then surrendering ourselves to him. It's turning toward heaven and turning your back on the world. Worship sets the table for communion with God. Many people have the notion that worship is limited to that time in a church service when you stand and sing, but really it's all that and more. Even if you can't sing a note, you can worship in the way you live your life. Worship is your love offering to a God who is so awesome we can't help but bow before him—figuratively and literally.

For about five years now, I have carried these helpful verses from the Bible in my wallet:

Therefore, I urge you, brothers, in view of God's mercy, to offer your bodies as living sacrifices, holy and pleasing to God—this is your spiritual act of worship. Do not conform any longer to the pattern of this world, but be transformed by the renewing of your mind. Then you will be able to test and approve what God's will is—his good, pleasing and perfect will. (Rom. 12:1–2)

Can you even imagine the concept of becoming a living sacrifice? That's what we need to work toward. But the best part is that, as usual, God has our best interests in mind. Our worship directed to God helps transform us in such a way that we can know his will for our lives. Wow.

Last thought: If you still don't get this, then find yourself a good Bible-centered church with a solid worship leader and a great band that really rocks. True, worship is more than music. But singing with gusto alongside hundreds of other authentic believers will help you understand the vertical nature of worship. It creates a sure connection between you and your Creator.

HEAVENLY FATHER, *my soul rejoices in you. You are so awesome, and yet you care for me. I want to offer each and every part of my body as a living sacrifice to you. Please, Lord, open my eyes to who you are. Reveal your will for my life so that I may worship you with even greater joy for all eternity. Amen.*

Then I looked and heard the voice of many angels, numbering thousands upon thousands, and ten thousand times ten thousand. They encircled the throne and the living creatures and the elders. In a loud voice they sang: "Worthy is the Lamb, who was slain, to receive power and wealth and wisdom and strength and honor and glory and praise!"
—Revelation 5:11–12

Day 16: Adoration. Contrition. Thanksgiving. Supplication.

God is not dead. I talked with him this morning.
—Bumper sticker

YEARS AGO, SOMEONE TAUGHT me about four kinds of prayer, which you can remember by referencing the word *ACTS* as a mnemonic device. *Adoration* is closely related to worship. *Contrition* is acknowledging our sinful condition and seeking forgiveness. *Thanksgiving* shows awareness that everything we have is on loan from a generous God. *Supplication* is bringing our requests to him. There are shelves of wonderful books on the topic of prayer, but if you're looking for a place to start, you can't go wrong using A-C-T-S.

The Lord's Prayer (aka the "Our Father") may be the perfect model for prayer. It was first presented by Jesus himself as "how you should pray," and you may be surprised to learn you can find it word-for-word in the gospel of Matthew, chapter 6. Not surprisingly, adoration, contrition, thanksgiving, and supplication are all woven into the Lord's Prayer. Check it out for yourself.

The Bible is filled with truths, instructions, warnings, and challenges on the topic of prayer: All prayers are always heard. "You will seek me and find me when you seek me with all your heart" (Jer. 29:13). All prayers are answered. "If you believe, you will receive whatever you ask for in prayer" (Matt. 21:22).

Be heartfelt and sincere. Don't try to impress God with fancy, repetitive prayers:

And when you pray, do not be like the hypocrites, for they love to pray standing in the synagogues and on the street corners to be seen by men. I tell you the truth, they have received their reward in full. But when you pray, go into your room, close the door and pray to your Father, who is unseen. Then your Father, who sees what is done in secret, will reward you. And when you pray, do not keep on babbling like pagans, for they think they will be heard because of their many words. Do not be like them, for your Father knows what you need before you ask him. (Matt. 6:5–8)

Prayer can rescue a nation. "If my people, who are called by my name, will humble themselves and pray and seek my face and turn from their wicked ways, then will I hear from heaven and will forgive their sin and will heal their land" (2 Chron. 7:14). Prayer should focus less on speaking and more on listening. "Guard your steps when you go to the house of God. Go near to listen rather than to offer the sacrifice of fools, who do not know that they do wrong. Do not be quick with your mouth, do not be hasty in your heart to utter anything before God. God is in heaven and you are on earth, so let your words be few" (Eccl. 5:1–2). Our entire lives should be an ongoing prayer. "Pray without ceasing" (1 Thess. 5:17 NASB).

Two last insights from an occasional prayer warrior.

First, never hesitate to pray for anything at any time. You can even ask God to help find a parking spot. Second, if you really want a more effective prayer life, then pray for a more effective prayer life. In other words, just pray.

HEAVENLY FATHER, *let my life be a prayer. Let my thought life be a prayer. Let my actions be prayers. Help me to come to you in gratitude, in humility, with an expectant heart, for I trust you know what's best for me. Amen.*

**The prayer of a righteous man
is powerful and effective.**
—James 5:16

Day 17: Basic Information Before Leaving Earth

There's no better book with which to defend
the Bible than the Bible itself.
—D. L. Moody

YES, THE BIBLE IS sometimes difficult to understand. Yes, it can seem repetitive or contradictory or irrelevant. Yes, scholars and teachers sometimes misinterpret passages of Scripture. But those are all human failings. The Bible itself is the only trustworthy and perfect instruction manual for life.

Consider this passage: "All Scripture is inspired by God and profitable for teaching, for reproof, for correction, for training in righteousness" (2 Tim. 3:16 NASB). Now, that's the Bible claiming that the Bible is valuable. A cynic might say,

"That doesn't prove anything. That's circular logic." But the Bible *does* prove itself to be infallible over and over again.

Bible historians, archaeologists, and apologists can present volumes of convincing evidence supporting the reliability of the Scriptures. Some of which I have even sorted through. For me, I've embraced three simple truths that have washed away any doubt I ever had.

Messianic prophecies

History shows that the Old Testament was written long before Jesus was born. But there are literally hundreds of prophecies in the Old Testament that point very specifically to where, when, and how Jesus would be born, live, die, and rise from the dead. For instance, seven hundred years before Christ, Micah 5:2 predicted the Messiah would come from a tiny town called Bethlehem. Isaiah predicted the virgin birth, Jesus' miracles, and exact circumstances of his crucifixion and burial.

Recent archeological discoveries

In each generation, secular scientists are stunned to uncover new evidence supporting the biblical record, while Christians stand by saying, "We knew it all along." In 1947, a Bedouin goatherd came upon a cave containing jars filled with ancient manuscripts. Those Dead Sea Scrolls confirmed the accuracy of much of today's Old Testament. For centuries, critics suggested that Old Testament cities such as Petra, Ubar, and Ebla were merely myths. But modern technology and determined archaeologists have found them buried in the desert sand. And the list goes on.

Personal confidence

I am a healthy skeptic. I consider myself a thinking Christian. The more I read and understand Scripture, the more it makes sense and the more useful it is to me as a husband, father, friend, businessman, and member of the local and world community. I feel confident when called to defend my faith—mostly because Christianity works. It's not just a set of arbitrary rules. It's all about my relationship with Jesus and this world he loves so much. I take it as a personal challenge when the Bible says, "Always be prepared to give an answer to everyone

who asks you to give the reason for the hope that you have. But do this with gentleness and respect" (1 Peter 3:15).

So may I suggest—with gentleness and respect—that you spend some serious time reading God's Word. Get a good study Bible. Start with the gospel of John. And then continue wherever the Lord leads. It will transform your life. But don't take my word for it. Take his Word.

HEAVENLY FATHER, *I desperately want to know you, your righteous laws, and your will for my life. And all of that is in your Word. Please Lord, give me a hunger for Scripture. Help me be consistent and diligent in the study of the Bible. Give me fresh joy each time I open your Word. Amen.*

**Your word is a lamp to my feet
and a light for my path.**
—Psalm 119:105

Day 18: Where's the Coffee?

See ya Friday a.m.
—The close of most e-mails from my small group leader

I AM NOT A morning person. Just ask Mike, Jim, Lu, Mark, George, Phil, Ronn, David, Jack, Jim, Jim, Kent, Mike, Ron, Mark, Terry, Dennis, Randy, Tom, Frank, Chris, Fred, and Mark. These are the guys with whom I have had the privilege of gathering each week for the last fifteen years or so. Usually on Friday mornings. Usually at 6:15. Usually at Colonial Restaurant. I've gone through four different leaders. And the roster has fluctuated from four to eleven guys.

Here's how it works for us. We stumble in groggily one at a time between 6:05 and 6:25 (except for Ron, who's always cheery). For about a half hour, between four and eight guys just like you catch up on life events: work, travel, kids' crises, kids' victories, illnesses, world news, business trends, church politics, and whatever else is on our minds. During that time, Jackie comes and takes our orders. Then we shift into a slightly more serious mode and dig into whatever book, devotional, or study guide we're doing.

The books we've read are not surprising. We've talked about identifying our love languages, living purpose-driven lives, and building a case for Christ. We've scribbled our way through study guides on a variety of topics and had some pretty heady discussions on C. S. Lewis's *The Screwtape Letters.* Some of the best studies we've done have simply been using our study Bibles to walk through different books of the Bible. We take a chapter a week and everyone gets a chance to pose a question or share an insight. Between studies—every couple months or so—we set aside a morning to go around the table with prayer requests.

It's not difficult or mysterious. But it is powerful. Most guys would never take the time to stop and consider these issues without being forced to. The best thing about that regular Friday morning event is that it gets me thinking about truths and people other than my own little world. It makes me less selfish. I actually care about these guys!

All of this to say, "Get into a small group." Join one or start one. If I can drag myself out of bed at 5:30 a.m. most Fridays, so can you. Or meet in the evening if you prefer.

Don't worry if you travel and might miss a few gatherings. Don't worry if you're shy. Don't worry if you're not a spiritual giant. It's actually advantageous if the members are not all the same age, same income, or same level of spiritual maturity. Jesus had a small group, which included guys who fished, collected taxes, and showed every kind of emotion including fear, doubt, anger, love, patriotism, greed, and courage. You should expect the same kind of diversity and intellectual stimulation from your group.

Over the years, I've had the privilege to see God work in the lives of some pretty great guys. Dave got suddenly laid off, but ended up with a job closer to home with a bigger, better company. Mark retired early from corporate life and threw himself into ministry.

Jay had a couple of books published. Jim got that promotion. Kent courageously downsized his house for the sake of his kids. We've celebrated babies, foster babies, and adoptions. Our teenagers are holding their own. Maybe best of all, Terry hasn't had a drink in four years. Gentlemen, I salute you all.

HEAVENLY FATHER, *thank you for the men you've brought into my life to challenge me, lift me up, advise me, and pray for me and my family. Give me the courage to tear down the walls I've built so that others can learn from my experiences and I can learn from theirs. Amen.*

Let us not give up meeting together, as some are in the habit of doing, but let us encourage one another—and all the more as you see the Day approaching.
—Hebrews 10:25

Day 19: Total Transparency

As iron sharpens iron, so one man sharpens another.
—Proverbs 27:17

IF GOD REALLY KNOWS what's best for us and has a wonderfully fulfilling plan for our lives, then we should be eager to surrender every corner of our lives to him. Here's an exercise to help you pray through a "surrender checklist":

My life is like a house. And I welcome Jesus into every room. I invite him into my living room, surrendering my relationship with my family. I invite him into my kitchen, surrendering my gluttony or other bad habits related to my physical self. I invite him into my workshop that I may use my hands to serve him. I invite him into the master bedroom that I may be an affirming, unselfish

husband. I invite him into my garage that he will accom-
pany me wherever I go, protecting my travels …

Using your home as a guide, you'll cover every area of your life as you welcome Jesus into each room. This is an easy exercise—until you get to that one dark closet into which Jesus is not invited. The one you're not proud of, yet you still go there on a regular basis. Identifying that dark closet and having the courage to bring your sinful condition into the light is one benefit of an accountability partner.

What's an accountability partner? He's a lot like you. Your accountability partner should be about the same age and spiritual maturity as you are. He's easy to talk to and will keep your word in confidence. The accountability concept is that you meet him for coffee or lunch every other week or so and open yourself up to questions.

First, catch up on life stuff—jobs, families, other top-of-mind issues. Don't waste time talking about sports, movies, or stock tips. After that, it gets a little tougher as your accountability partner asks a short list of questions the two of you have customized to your areas of struggle, such as:

- How have you done with anger since we last met?
- How have you done with your spending habits?

- Have you been keeping your word?
- Have you made time for your kids?
- How's your prayer time?
- How many days since we last met have you spent at least fifteen minutes in the Bible?
- Did you call Jeff and ask for forgiveness yet?
- On your business trip last week, did you watch any adult movies in your motel room?

Most of the questions are the same each time you meet. All of them are very personal, and that can be a little threatening. But your accountability partner isn't really asking the questions. You are. You have given him permission to hold you accountable. And if you're open and vulnerable, you will soon take great strides in opening those dark closets to God's light.

Jim Nicodem, a pastor in St. Charles, Illinois, suggests that accountability partners finish with one last question that can help reveal your most secret area of sin. After completing those tough questions, simply ask, "Have you lied to me during any of your answers?"

Men, it's time to get real. Meeting with an accountability partner on a regular basis is a powerful way to start.

HEAVENLY FATHER, *there are areas in my life I struggle to surrender completely. The idea of being honest with a brother in Christ about the sin in my life is intimidating. But if you place a name on my heart, I'll pursue an accountability relationship with him. Please guide me in this area. Amen.*

Two are better than one, because they
have a good return for their work: If one falls
down, his friend can help him up. But pity the
man who falls and has no one to help him up!
—Ecclesiastes 4:9–10

Day 20: You Can't Outgive God

We make a living by what we get,
we make a life by what we give.
—Winston Churchill

DIG DEEPER INTO YOUR spiritual toolbox and you'll find a valuable tool that will draw you closer to God. Yet, it remains misunderstood, underused, and even abused. It's tithing. The dreaded "T" word. To clear up some long-held misconceptions about it, let's try a little Q & A exercise.

Isn't tithing an Old Testament concept?

Yes! God's people seemed to accept it unconditionally. *A tithe of everything from the land, whether grain from the soil or fruit from the trees, belongs to the LORD. (Lev. 27:30; see also Deut. 14:22; Neh. 12:44)*

Does it still apply?

Well, Jesus was quite clear that the teachers of the Old Testament law were still to be honored and that we "must obey them and do everything they tell you" (Matt. 23:3). With an even stronger reminder, Jesus said he did not come to abolish the law, but to fulfill it (see Matt. 5:17–20).

But is tithing actually referenced in the New Testament?

Yes, Jesus talks about tithing in Matthew 23 and Luke 18. In Hebrews 7, there's a great history lesson about Abraham's tithing to his spiritual leader. Interestingly, most New Testament references to tithing confirm how important it is … but also reaffirm that it's not enough.

So tithing doesn't get you a reserved spot in heaven?

Nope, sorry. Tithing is in the same category as "good works." For sure, a heart that is generous with time, talent, and treasure is wonderful evidence of your faith. But only accepting Christ as your Savior leads to salvation.

And where did that 10 percent figure come from?

Tithe means "tenth." But that's just a starting point. Jesus talked several times about how we need to go beyond what the Pharisees did. To one rich young ruler, Jesus even says, "Sell *everything* you have and give to the poor, and you will have treasure in heaven" (Mark 10:21, emphasis added). That's not 10 percent, it's 100 percent!

Okay, what's in it for me?

Well, how about these promises from God's perfect Word: *A generous man will prosper; he who refreshes others will himself be refreshed. (Prov. 11:25; see also 2 Cor. 9:6; Luke 6:38)*

So if I give I'm going to become wealthy!

Yes, but not necessarily in banking terms. Your deepest needs will be met. You and your family will prosper. You may very well find yourself with less money, but more satisfaction.

And how do I explain the idea of tithing to my wife?

It's an attitude change she will very likely applaud. You're actually putting God in charge of your finances.

Tell me again why tithing works?

Everything is God's anyway. He's quite generously letting you keep 90 percent. Besides, God doesn't need your money. He wants your heart. As one of God's children, he is going to take care of your every need. So jump in with a full 10 percent. Go ahead and try to outgive God!

HEAVENLY FATHER, *it's becoming so clear that the way to free myself from financial anxiety is to put you in charge. Give me courage to take this step of faith and begin tithing. You are truly a loving, generous God. Amen.*

Each man should give what he has decided in his heart to give, not reluctantly or under compulsion, for God loves a cheerful giver.
—2 Corinthians 9:7

Day 21: Investing Your Talents

"It is high time that the ideal of success
should be replaced by the ideal of service."
—Albert Einstein

WHEN'S THE LAST TIME you read the parable of the talents? In Matthew 25:14–30, Jesus tells the story specifically to warn us that he is coming back and will expect us to have made good use of the gifts and abilities given to us by God.

But for men who are not afraid of a little hard work, the parable has a secondary significance. If you read between the lines, you'll see it's about the joys and rewards of servanthood. Read all twelve verses from the gospel of Matthew and decide for yourself.

It's not a coincidence that the word for money in this parable is "talent." You see, we all have God-given talents. Unless they are used specifically to help build the kingdom of God, you are not giving God a maximum return on his investment. He'll be disappointed. You'll miss out on his blessing. And—yikes!—you may even experience some weeping and gnashing of teeth.

Worst of all, if you waste your talents you'll be living a life of unsettled incompleteness. After all, we were created to serve and worship God. I spent years writing TV commercials, radio spots, and ads for a major advertising agency. At first I thought it was my dream job, but real satisfaction didn't come until I began using my gifts on behalf of Christian publishers and ministries.

Certainly you don't have to quit your job to work in full-time ministry. We desperately need Christians to be salt and light in the secular workforce. But if you have a talent for songwriting, some of your tunes should be worship and praise songs. If you have a talent for administration, volunteer to help coordinate the workload at a local shelter or ministry headquarters. If you're a master tradesman, then you might find satisfaction serving God in a handyman ministry.

As we've already seen, God doesn't need our help. It's you and I who need to give back to God in gratitude and be part of something bigger than ourselves. After surrendering even just part of our lives in sacrificial service, it will be music to our ears to hear God say, "Well done, good and faithful servant! You have been faithful with a few things; I will put you in charge of many things. Come and share your master's happiness!" (Matt. 25:21).

HEAVENLY FATHER, *thank you for the talents you have given me. Help me first to recognize those gifts, both large and small. Please show me where and how to use those gifts to help expand your kingdom here on earth. Amen.*

"For we are His workmanship, created in Christ Jesus for good works, which God prepared beforehand so that we would walk in them."
—Ephesians 2:10 NASB

Day 22: Got Spirit?

And I will ask the Father, and he will give you another
Counselor to be with you forever—the Spirit of truth.
—John 14:16–17

IN THE OLD TESTAMENT book of Isaiah, the prophet foretold of the birth of Christ and wrote that he would be called "Wonderful Counselor" (Isa. 9:6). Seven hundred years later, that's exactly what happened.

Then at the Last Supper, the Wonderful Counselor himself patiently explained many vital concepts of the Christian faith to his disciples, including the earth-changing events that would unfold over the following three days. Imagine the disciples' concern and puzzlement when Jesus revealed that he was going to the Father, but would send "another

Counselor." Another counselor? How could anyone possibly replace Jesus, their living, breathing, walking friend who taught them and guided them with such clarity?

Jesus calmed their fears and eased their grief by saying, "But I tell you the truth: It is for your good that I am going away. Unless I go away, the Counselor will not come to you; but if I go, I will send him to you. When he comes, he will convict the world of guilt in regard to sin and righteousness and judgment" (John 16:7–8).

Sure enough, the second chapter of Acts records the coming of the Holy Spirit at Pentecost, and Christians have been blessed by his supernatural guidance ever since. This new Counselor's purpose is to help us recognize right and wrong, to convict us when we fall short, and to empower us to act boldly in the face of injustice or evil.

I believe the Holy Spirit led Rosa Parks to hold her seat on that Montgomery, Alabama, city bus in 1955. She knew she was breaking the law when she refused to give up her seat for a white passenger, but somehow she also knew she was doing the right thing. She later wrote, "I felt the presence of God on the bus and heard his quiet voice as I sat there waiting for the police." Mrs. Parks didn't set out to become a heroic symbol of the civil rights movement, but that's what happens when you allow yourself to be led by the Spirit.

I believe the Holy Spirit also instructed Todd Beamer to help lead the charge up the aisle of the hijacked jetliner on September 11, 2001. When that plane nosedived into a Pennsylvania field, Beamer and his brave colleagues saved the lives of hundreds of other Americans in some high-profile building targeted for destruction. His courage and rallying cry of "Let's roll" still resonates in the grateful hearts of a nation that had quite a few heroes that day. No terrorist attack can ever claim victory when the Holy Spirit is at work.

I believe every authentic Christian is guided every moment of every day by the indwelling of the Holy Spirit. It's just that some of us choose not to follow his counsel. And it's also worth noting that the Holy Spirit is not just a tool in your spiritual toolbox. He's a real person you can count as an unending source of comfort, wisdom, intercession, and truth. Just as Jesus promised.

HEAVENLY FATHER, *I accept your lordship in my life. I accept the sacrifice your Son made on the cross on my behalf. And I accept the guidance of the Holy Spirit in every possible circumstance. I trust that in following the guidance of the Spirit I will find truth, freedom, courage, and conviction. Amen.*

**But when he, the Spirit of truth, comes,
he will guide you into all truth.**
—John 16:13

Section 4 · TURNING THE CORNER

Day 23: The Big Picture

There is a God and you're not Him.
—T-shirt quote

SO HERE WE ARE. You're more than halfway through this forty-day devotional. We've helped you uncover and confess some of your worst habits, and we've suggested quite a few valuable tools that can help you get your act together. Now we're ready to turn the corner.

The goal is not just to make you a better you. It's to make you the best you possible. But there's a problem. You don't even know what that looks like. Your best life is far beyond your human comprehension. It's over the horizon of your imagination. Still, you need to realize that God loves you without limits and has a perfect plan for you to reach your full potential. He has a vision for you as a husband, father, friend, and saint. He wants you to experience spiritual growth, confidence, passion, fulfillment, and joy in the journey.

God sees the big picture. And we need to trust his guidance.

In his book *Right from Wrong*, apologist Josh McDowell paints a vivid word picture of how God's perspective works. Josh explains how the choices we make throughout life are like a boy stuck in a maze at a carnival. He keeps making wrong turns and getting farther and farther from the goal line because from inside the maze he doesn't have enough data to make the best choices. However, when his dad climbs a tall ladder and looks down on the maze, he easily discerns the way out and guides the boy with easy-to-follow instructions, "Turn right, take the second left, follow this corridor," etc. In other words, the dad sees the big picture.

Just so, our heavenly Father looks down and sees all of time and space—past, present, and future—at the same instant. He sees the garden of Eden, the garden of Gethsemane, and the tomatoes in your backyard. At this very moment, God sees your first cries as a newborn, your next birthday, and your last breath. That's his job. Our job is to trust him.

Frankly, it's a good thing God has limited our vision because, honestly, we couldn't handle life otherwise. Great joys and great sorrows lie ahead for all of us. They come in a flash and impact us forever. If we saw the big picture and knew everything that waited around the next corner, it would blow our minds. We'd run for cover or freeze in our tracks.

Yes, God gave us free will. We can choose to follow him or not. His omnipresence, omniscience, and omnipotence cannot be denied. But still many of us—indeed, most of us—choose to follow our own feeble sensibilities.

Therefore, I would like to echo the challenge the Old Testament hero Joshua gave to his followers in his final message: "Choose for yourselves this day whom you will serve.... But as for me and my household, we will serve the LORD" (Josh. 24:15).

HEAVENLY FATHER, *thank you for revealing to me only as much as I can handle. Thank you for giving me a vision for your vision. I trust that you will forgive me for my past mistakes, love me in my present state, and guide me in all my future days. Yes, I will follow you. Amen.*

**As the heavens are higher than the earth,
so are my ways higher than your ways
and my thoughts than your thoughts.**
—Isaiah 55:9

Day 24: Pictures of Love

But God demonstrates his own love for us in this:
While we were still sinners, Christ died for us.
—Romans 5:8

A RESPECTFUL, SENSITIVE YOUNG boy turns into a rebellious teenager and breaks his parents' hearts. In the middle of the night, he comes home drunk and passes out across his bed. His mother slips out of her own bed and minutes later her husband goes to the kitchen expecting to find her crying alone. Instead he discovers her at the boy's bedside gently stroking his matted hair. "What are you doing?" her husband asks. She replies, "He won't let me love him when he's awake."

That's a picture of unconditional love. Here's another.

A son demands an early inheritance, leaves home, and squanders it all on depraved living. Starving and living with pigs, he realizes he would be better off back at home. But he also realizes he has given up the right to be part of the family he left behind. So he begins the long walk home. Off in the distance, the father sees the prodigal son approaching and runs to the boy with open arms to welcome him back. You see, where sin had increased, grace had increased all the more. A life without boundaries was met by a love without boundaries.

Here's another picture of unconditional love that's even more incredible.

God creates us. He loves us. We reject him. He still loves us. God sends his Son to teach us how to live. We kill him. God still loves us. God uses Jesus' blood to wash our sins away so that we can enter his kingdom without blemish.

To further make my point, here's a very personal picture of unconditional love.

God creates you. He loves you. You reject him. He still loves you. God sends his Son to teach you how to live. You kill him. God still loves you. God uses Jesus' blood to wash your sins away so that you can enter his kingdom without blemish.

It's true, you didn't wield the whip that tore at his skin or hammer the spikes into his hands. But always remember, your sin and mine was the reason he died. And by the way, God knew all this was going to happen even before the creation of the world. How do you respond to a love like that? As the Bible says, "We love Him because He first loved us" (1 John 4:19 NKJV).

HEAVENLY FATHER, *whenever I consider your grandeur, it still blows me away to think that you care about me. I know I can never love with the kind of unconditional love that you have. But help me try. Please, Lord, help me try. Amen.*

For God so loved the world that he gave his one and only Son, that whoever believes in him shall not perish but have eternal life.
—John 3:16

Day 25: When Two Become One

Happy wife, happy life.
—Jeff Allen

IF YOU'RE NOT MARRIED, you may consider skipping today's devotional. But don't, because this information will be useful to you. It's always fascinating to consider how often God's way seems to be the exact opposite of what the world is saying. Our culture's approach to marriage these days is a tragic example.

Have you ever been to a wedding that featured a recited or printed excerpt from Kahlil Gibran's *The Prophet?* For some reason, brides in recent decades have a misguided fascination with the words of the Lebanese poet who immigrated to the United States and in 1923 wrote a deeply flawed description of marriage. Here is an excerpt you may recognize:

But let there be spaces in your togetherness,

   And let the winds of the heavens dance between you.

   Love one another but make not a bond of love:

   Let it rather be a moving sea between the shores of your souls.

   Fill each other's cup but drink not from one cup.

   Give one another of your bread but eat not from the same loaf.

   Sing and dance together and be joyous, but let each one of you be alone.

Marriage is not about making sure there are "spaces in your togetherness." Despite what Gibran wrote, a successful marriage is very much about "making a bond of love," drinking from "one cup," and eating from "the same loaf." (Ask my wonderful and patient wife, Rita. I've been stealing food from her plate in restaurants for more than twenty-five years.)

As they head down the aisle, every bride (and groom) I've ever met is sincerely hoping to find unity, commitment, and mutual appreciation in marriage—the kind of marriage described throughout the Bible:

*For this reason a man will leave his father and mother
and be united to his wife, and they will become one flesh.
(Gen. 2:24)*

*Marriage should be honored by all, and the marriage bed
kept pure. (Heb. 13:4)*

Enjoy life with your wife, whom you love. (Eccl. 9:9)

*Husbands, in the same way be considerate as you live
with your wives. (1 Peter 3:7)*

Men, it's all about finding one good woman, becoming
one flesh, and staying together no matter what. It's pretty
simple, really. Put her needs before yours.

But what if you're a selfish oaf? Well, then think of it this
way. Pouring loving-kindness and consideration into her life
will help her become a wife of noble character, and you will
be the one reaping all kinds of great benefits.

In your community

*Her husband is respected at the city gate, where he takes
his seat among the elders of the land. (Prov. 31:23)*

In your cash flow

She sets about her work vigorously; her arms are strong

for her tasks. She sees that her trading is profitable and her lamp does not go out at night. (Prov. 31:17–18)

In your bedroom

Rejoice in the wife of your youth … may her breasts satisfy you always, may you ever be captivated by her love. (Prov. 5:18–19)

These verses prove God has our best interests in mind.

HEAVENLY FATHER, *I know that to become one with my wife I will need to invest in her physically, emotionally, and spiritually. Help me see and appreciate everything good about her. Help me confess my failures and be the kind of husband she needs me to be. Amen.*

"He who loves his wife loves himself."
—Ephesians 5:28

Day 26: Anticipatory Parenting

An ounce of prevention is worth a pound of cure.
—Benjamin Franklin

YOU CAN'T DO A devotional for men without setting aside at least one chapter on fatherhood. So here it is. And here's a great parenting secret: Be aware of your kids' needs. Actually, be so aware of your kids' needs that you know what they need before they do.

A few examples of "anticipatory parenting" may help. Have a fresh diaper and several baby wipes ready BEFORE you open the dirty diaper. Plug up the electrical outlets BEFORE your toddler starts crawling. Check out the schools BEFORE you move into a new neighborhood.

Does this make sense? Sure it does. But it's not always

easy. To stay one step ahead of your kids, you need to spend time with them, know where they're headed, and know what is going on in their sweet little heads.

Anticipatory parenting is not just about preventing disasters. It can also help you be a hero in the eyes of your child. Play catch with your kids BEFORE baseball tryouts and they have a better chance of making the team. Have a stash of markers and poster boards in your closet BEFORE they come to you Sunday night at seven p.m. frantic about a project due the next day. Put their birthdays, concerts, and game schedules on your calendar BEFORE any other appointments so you can make most of them.

The importance of anticipatory parenting becomes even more obvious as the kids get older. Have your young teenagers commit to sexual purity BEFORE their first date. If you wait until their friends are already sexually active, it's way too late. The phrase "Just say no" to drugs may seem a little corny, but it's your job to help your kids find ways to say no BEFORE they are confronted with that decision.

Make sure they understand the concept of defensive driving BEFORE they get their license. Probably the most important skill you can teach them behind the wheel is to leave a long interval between their front bumper and the car ahead. As they scan the road looking for potholes, brake lights, kids running out from between parked cars, and bone-head drivers, they're actually learning anticipatory driving.

The most quoted Bible verse on parenting is really all about anticipatory parenting. "Train a child in the way he should go, and when he is old he will not turn from it" (Prov. 22:6). Of course, children make their own choices and parents shouldn't hold themselves responsible every time their kids mess up. But ask any parent with a child who flunked out, tuned out, or got into a ton of trouble. Those parents will almost always say, "I didn't see it coming."

Dads, they grow up so fast. Don't miss out. And the time you invest today will help you see into their future. Can you envision them at school tomorrow? Can you see them launching a career or starting their own family? Most important, are they ready to face eternity?

HEAVENLY FATHER, *my natural instinct is to spend time with my kids. But too many things distract me from making that investment. Help me spend these short years getting to know and appreciate these children. You have given me a gift and a responsibility. Show me how to help them build a future of loving and serving you. Amen.*

Fathers, do not exasperate your children; instead, bring them up in the training and instruction of the Lord.
—Ephesians 6:4

Day 27: A Not So Beautiful Day in the Neighborhood

The Bible tells us to love our neighbors, and also to love our enemies; probably because they are generally the same people!
–G. K. Chesterton

YOU'RE STUCK WITH YOUR family and they're stuck with you. You have to be nice to people at work because your cash flow depends on it. But what about your neighbors? What if you just don't care for them? What if their dog digs up your rosebushes, their teenagers play raucous heavy metal at two a.m., they have a rusted-out pickup parked on the edge of your property line, and their trees drip sap on the hood of your car?

Well, like every other relationship you have, the Bible

has much to say about getting along with people who are tough to get along with. Your enemies will have to settle up with God at a later date, but for now your response is—once again—to do the opposite of what the world might suggest. In a simple phrase, kill 'em with kindness.

If your enemy is hungry, feed him; if he is thirsty, give him something to drink. In doing this, you will heap burning coals on his head. (Rom. 12:20)

What a great image that is. Your abrasive neighbors may or may not know how irritating they are. They may enjoy being obnoxious or possibly they're oblivious to how they upset the neighborhood serenity. In any case, they probably rub just about everybody they meet the wrong way and don't have too many authentic friendships. Suddenly you come along and treat them with absolute love and respect. Without a doubt, your actions will get their attention.

It might take a while, but they will ultimately acknowledge your good deeds and give glory to God. That's the reason Jesus said, "Love your enemies and pray for those who persecute you."

It may be hard to admit, but God loves your neighbors just as much as he loves you. It would be nice to be his favorite, but that's not the way it works. Besides, we are all far from perfect. We mess up all the time. That's the sinful nature of man. As authentic Christians, we should do our best to keep our own dogs leashed, keep our own teens respectful, and keep our own yards tidy. But when we fail, we need to be the first to ask forgiveness and work the hardest to change our ways. Our witness depends on it.

Bottom line: Never give a nonbeliever a reason to view you as a hypocrite. You may be the only Christian he knows.

HEAVENLY FATHER, *like the Good Samaritan, help me to see a need and fill it. Help me love my neighbor, no matter what the world says. Help my life shine so that others are attracted to you. Amen.*

Live such good lives among the pagans that, though they accuse you of doing wrong, they may see your good deeds and glorify God on the day he visits us.

—1 Peter 2:12

Day 28: Back to Square One

If Christ's lordship does not disrupt our lordship, then the reality
of our conversion must be questioned.
—Charles Colson

TIME FOR A LITTLE vital soul searching. As you've been journeying with this devotional over the last few weeks, have you been feeling a little lost? Are you thinking that although you've picked up a few nuggets of insight and practical advice, much of this content is not clicking for you?

Did you dutifully read the chapters that identified your sinful condition, but felt no conviction to change? Did you understand the importance of Bible reading, prayer, and/or tithing, but think "That's not my style"? Do you appreciate God's perspective, but figure you'd rather work it all out on your own? Did you silently decide you're already doing pretty well as a husband, father, and neighbor?

Well, then … you may not have taken the vital step of inviting Jesus into your heart. You may have spent the last few weeks, maybe your entire life, fooling yourself. Is that possible? Here are several tests to help you find out.

Check your actions. Do they follow God's laws?

The man who says, "I know him," but does not do what he commands is a liar, and the truth is not in him. But if anyone obeys his word, God's love is truly made complete in him. (1 John 2:4–5)

Check your guilt level. Are you convicted each time you sin?

If you are not disciplined (and everyone undergoes discipline), then you are illegitimate children and not true sons. (Heb. 12:8)

Check your hunger for the Bible. Does it speak to your heart?

The law from your mouth is more precious to me than thousands of pieces of silver and gold. (Ps. 119:72)

If you're not absolutely positive that you've accepted Jesus as your Savior, you can take care of that right now.

It doesn't cost anything. And it's just between you and God. All you really need is a clear head and a sincere heart.

So here it goes. Read these words. Understand them. Accept them. And then speak them to God.

Dear God, I want to know you personally. But my sin keeps me from you, prevents me from my best life here on earth, and will keep me from spending eternity with you in heaven. I know someone has to pay the penalty for that sin—and it should be me. But because you love me, you have provided the way out. You sent Jesus, who never sinned, to die on the cross and pay the penalty in my place. That gift is free. All I have to do is truly desire to stop sinning, believe in Jesus who died and rose from the dead, and ask Him to guide my life from now on. Lord, I choose right now to become a child of God. Please come into my life. Amen.

If you prayed that prayer for the first time, then welcome to the family of God! If you have not yet, you're missing out on the greatest adventure there is. As a new believer, don't expect to feel different—although you might. But you can expect to experience some new desires and insights. God is now your Father, Jesus your brother, and the Holy Spirit your guide.

I suggest that you now do two things: (1) Tell someone about this decision you've made, and (2) go back over the "Spiritual Toolbox" section (Days 15–22) because all those tools are now ready and waiting for you to use.

HEAVENLY FATHER, *thanks for creating me and thanks for rescuing me. Amen.*

**Behold, I stand at the door and knock;
if anyone hears my voice and opens the door,
I will come in to him**
—Revelation 3:20 KJV

Day 29: When Heaven Applauds

Christianity has not been tried and found wanting.
It has been found difficult and left untried.
—*G. K. Chesterton*

AS A NEW CREATION in Christ, the way you perceive the world has totally changed. You should now see the world as a field of battle and a field ripe for harvest. At the same time, the world also looks at you in a totally different light. And it's not pretty or pleasant. Believe it or not, authentic Christians should expect to experience some animosity from the general public. Jesus comes right out and says, "I have chosen you out of the world. That is why the world hates you" (John 15:19).

That idea may be a little confusing. After years of

schmoozing, winning friends, and picking up the checks in restaurants, you are now the odd man out. So how do you deal with that? Well, since you've already tasted the living water, why not jump all the way in? When confronted with challenges and tough decisions, go ahead and ask yourself, "What would Jesus do?" When your buddies invite you to go all-night bar hopping, take a pass. When your work colleagues are all padding their expense accounts, be extra meticulous with yours. When the pornography gets passed around or the cursing escalates, excuse yourself.

If being a man of integrity means that you suffer a few cheap shots, that's actually a good thing. If you don't get invited to the next bash at the strip clubs, be glad. If you get labeled as a party pooper, wear that badge with honor.

In the Sermon on the Mount, Jesus said, "Count yourselves blessed every time people put you down or throw you out or speak lies about you to discredit me. What it means is that the truth is too close for comfort and they are uncomfortable. You can be glad when that happens—give a cheer, even!—for though they don't like it, I do! And all heaven applauds" (Matt. 5:11–12 MSG).

So do you want to hear the sound of heaven clapping? Then speak and live the truth courageously—even if it is a little too close for comfort for some people. It's okay, because if folks put you down, you can count yourself blessed.

If it still seems too hard, consider this. Most of those people who mock Christians are secretly envious that you have your act together. They want what you have. And the longer you stay strong, the greater your witness. Sometime when you least expect it, the guy who has been delivering the biggest insults will come up to you when no one else is around and say, "I'm having a problem and I need some advice. I don't know where else to turn." The best part is, as a student of the Bible, you'll be able to give him some answers that work!

One other thing. If you're taking a lot of grief on the job, with your friends, or with your family, there is a place you can go where you won't be persecuted for your faith. If you don't have a good church that teaches truths from the Bible and supports you in your stand for righteousness, then find one ASAP. At my church, there's heavenly applause every week.

HEAVENLY FATHER, *I am looking forward to eternity with you. But right now I want to live for you. Help me be salt and light so that I may draw others to you. Give me courage and wisdom to defend my faith. Help me love everyone you put in my path. Amen.*

Always be prepared to give an answer to everyone who asks you to give the reason for the hope that you have. But do this with gentleness and respect.

—1 Peter 3:15

Day 30: Sand in Your Sandals

The saints are the sinners who keep on going.
—Robert Louis Stevenson

A HUSBAND AND WIFE are driving down the road and after miles of silence she sighs and says, "Remember when we were young and we always used to sit right next to each other in the car?" After a moment, the husband replies, "I remember. But you know, I haven't moved."

It's an old story (written way before seat-belt laws) but the point is well taken. When we're in a spiritual desert— feeling lost and far away from God—we need to acknowledge that God didn't move, we did. He never changes. He is still eager to spend time with you. His inspired Word is gathering dust on the other side of the room. He knows where you are and what you need.

God's power is always available to us, but we may for some reason have pulled the plug and we're now having a hard time finding the outlet again or untangling the extension cord. There's also a good chance that we were fooled into experimenting with another energy source, but it just couldn't match the staying power of the Creator of the universe. We're left feeling lost in the desert.

So how do you reconnect when you feel abandoned by God? First, realize that every emotion you have was also experienced by Jesus. He knew his death on the cross was part of a heavenly plan, but still Jesus cried, "My God, my God, why have you forsaken me?" (Matt. 27:46). Second, have faith that it's a temporary condition. The Israelites wandered in the desert for forty years, but eventually they reached the Promised Land.

Third, embrace your exile to the desert as a season of dormancy preparing you for explosive growth and impact. Before he performed any recorded miracles, Jesus voluntarily spent forty days fasting in the desert enduring Satan's well-documented temptations. The next three years marked the most important period in the history of the world.

Fourth, realize that there is life in the desert. Sure, it seems desolate, but a teeming community of reptiles, small mammals, spiders, and other creatures burrow just beneath the surface of the sand. Cacti thrive on very little moisture. Oases spring up out of nowhere. Desert dweller John the Baptist fulfilled prophecy and did some of his most important work while strolling from one dusty town to another. He was "a voice of one calling in the desert, 'Prepare the way for the Lord, make straight paths for him'" (Mark 1:3). And that was before sunglasses and sunscreen.

So next time you find yourself in a spiritual desert, stop your whining and enjoy the feel of the sand between your toes and the sun on your face. Because in the very near future you may be put back to work. God may be preparing you for great things or he may ask you to be a loud, clear voice announcing the coming of Christ right where you are.

HEAVENLY FATHER, *I learn much from mountaintop experiences. But I know I can learn even more from surviving difficult seasons in the desert. Thank you for giving me the living water of your Son, Jesus, that I may never be thirsty and without purpose in life. Amen.*

**Even though I walk through the valley
of the shadow of death, I will fear no evil,
for you are with me; your rod and staff,
they comfort me.**
—Psalm 23:4

Day 31: Rocks, Brambles, and Tunnels

God will not look you over for medals, degrees,
or diplomas, but for scars.
—Elbert Hubbard

MOST OF THE ILLUSTRATIONS in the book *Once Upon a Tandem* are whimsical woodcut drawings just a little larger than postage stamps. The illustrations by Rex Bohn help tell the story of a lone traveler riding a two-seated bicycle through life. He passes many suspicious-looking hitchhikers, but finally stops for an unnamed stranger. On the rear seat, the new passenger is a strong pedaler and even whispers directions that lead to shortcuts and smooth roads.

The driver has some fears and regrets, but his purpose in life finally comes into focus when he stops the tandem bike and invites the hitchhiker to take the front seat—handlebars and all. Allegorically, that's when he finally surrenders his life to Jesus. The graphic images of the scenic routes, detours, and mountaintops are delightful. But readers tell me the most striking moment of the book is when you turn from page ninety-nine and see an unexpected drawing that fills the next two-page spread. It's a long dark tunnel with just a sliver of light at the end. That's when astute readers realize that the Christian life is not all sweet and easy. You're going to go through dark tunnels. You're going to "ride down perilous roads strewn with rocks and brambles."

As a matter of fact, the Bible actually promises that we are going to suffer for our faith. But don't worry, that only makes us stronger.

> *After you have suffered for a little while, the God of all grace, who called you to His eternal glory in Christ, will Himself perfect, confirm, strengthen and establish you.* (1 Peter 5:10 *NASB*)

So when you invite Jesus to join you on your journey down the road of life, remember to listen to his direction, give him total control over the handlebars, and trust him to take you places you never dreamed of going. But also know that you may end up on some roads that are a little bumpy and a little frightening.

Yes, you may sometimes feel like you're hanging on for dear life. Yes, sometimes he may ask you to pedal—even though he doesn't really need your help. And no, the handlebars on the backseat of a tandem bike don't steer at all. But that's all part of the adventure. As long as you have chosen Christ as your Savior, there's always light at the end of the tunnel.

HEAVENLY FATHER, *accepting your gift of grace was the most difficult and most important decision of my life. Assured of my salvation, I have a new freedom that I never expected. But I realize I still have areas of my life to surrender to you. I want my life to be totally sanctified so I can know your perfect will and experience all your glory. Amen.*

**Trust in the LORD with all your heart
and lean not on your own understanding;
in all your ways acknowledge him,
and he will make your paths straight.**
—Proverbs 3:5–6

Section 5: BIG IDEAS

Day 32: 490 Times

Christians aren't perfect. Just forgiven.
—Bumper sticker

IT'S THE HOME STRETCH. You've got heaven applaud-
ing, you've maneuvered through some rough spots, and
things are even getting better at home. You're ready for
some lofty theological principles. Not too many. Just the
basics, including today's topic: forgiveness.

You know, I'm actually very good at asking forgiveness.
Maybe that's because I've had a lot of practice.

I've apologized to umpires when I yell too much at ball
games. I've apologized to all five of my kids when deadlines
are nipping at my heels and they inadvertently derail my
train of thought. I've apologized for taking corners too fast

and laying down Scrabble tiles too slowly. I've apologized for sometimes serving lukewarm pop and lukewarm pizza.

And, most important, I apologize to my wife on a regular basis for being wrong—even when I'm not 100 percent sure that I am.

Asking forgiveness is a great tool for keeping the peace. It's a great way to say, "Please give me another chance." Asking forgiveness and giving forgiveness is what Christians do. In the Lord's Prayer, Jesus reminds us that we regularly need to ask God for forgiveness and to forgive others who have done us wrong (see Matt. 6:12). Jesus also said that when someone who has sinned against you truly repents, you should forgive him not seven times, but seventy *times* seven! (See Matt. 18:22 NKJV.)

Probably the best reason to have a forgiving heart is because it gets you right with God. Jesus said, "And when you stand praying, if you hold anything against anyone, forgive him, so that your Father in heaven may forgive you your sins" (Mark 11:25).

But Jesus didn't just teach forgiveness; he modeled it. On the cross, Jesus—once again—proves his love for humankind by turning to heaven and saying, "Father, forgive them, for they do not know what they are doing" (Luke 23:34).

While sorting out all this talk about forgiveness, there seem to be several avenues to pursue. When we hurt another person, we need to apologize. When we get hurt, we need to be eager to forgive those who have hurt us. And when we disappoint God, we need to go to him with a broken heart and ask his forgiveness. When we do, he erases that sin from his memory, casting our sins away "as far as the east is from the west" (Ps. 103:12).

So who have you wronged, what grudges are you holding, what walls have you built, and what sins are you still denying? Some guys reading this right now haven't spoken to a particular friend or family member for decades because they didn't understand the power and personal satisfaction of giving and receiving forgiveness. What are you waiting for?

Forgiveness is a huge theme throughout the New Testament. Meditate on these words Paul wrote from inside a prison cell to the Colossian church: "Clothe yourselves with compassion, kindness, humility, gentleness and patience. Bear with each other and forgive whatever grievances you may have against one another. Forgive as the Lord forgave you. And over all these virtues put on love, which binds them all together in perfect unity" (Col. 3:12–14).

HEAVENLY FATHER, *I make so many mistakes it's hard to keep track. Still, I let my pride and stubbornness keep me from making things right. Soften my heart, Lord, so I can experience the joy and freedom of asking, receiving, and extending forgiveness. Give me courage to extend the hand of peace today. Amen.*

Get rid of all bitterness, rage and anger, brawling and slander, along with every form of malice.
Be kind and compassionate to one another, forgiving each other, just as in Christ God forgave you.
—Ephesians 4:31–32

Day 33: Washing Feet

Christ's deeds and examples are commandments
of what we should do.
—John Wycliffe

IMAGINE A BOARD OF directors meeting for a Fortune 500 company during which the CEO pulls out a basin of water and a towel and tenderly washes the feet of his top twelve board members. Unless it's some kind of publicity stunt, it's just not going to happen.

Now imagine the God of the universe washing your feet. That did happen. The gospel of John records the remarkable event in chapter 13 when Jesus washed and dried the dusty feet of the twelve disciples at the Last Supper. Know this: If you had been there, he would have washed your feet, too. Why would Jesus do something so outrageous? Perhaps a side benefit was to rid the dining hall of twenty-four dirty, stinky feet. But his real purpose was to be a model of sacrificial love. As he finished his humble task, Jesus explained:

Now that I, your Lord and Teacher, have washed your feet, you also should wash one another's feet. I have set you an example that you should do as I have done for you. (John 13:14–15)

This kind of sacrificial love can also be described with the oxymoron "servant leader." (An oxymoron is composed of two words that go together but seem to contradict each other: jumbo shrimp, disco music, political science, nice cat, virtual reality.) Does the term "servant leader" make any sense at all? It does when we consider that Jesus once again demonstrates how his way of doing things is the opposite of what the world expects. The Pharisees were waiting for a mighty warrior king. What they got was a Galilean carpenter who invited children to sit on his lap. They were confused. They were angry. If they had been quiet, they would have heard Jesus explain the relationship of servanthood to leadership.

Whoever wants to become great among you must be your servant, and whoever wants to be first must be your slave—just as the Son of Man did not come to be served, but to serve, and to give his life as a ransom for many. (Matt. 20:26–28)

In your role as a boss, coach, teacher, husband, father, uncle, or any position of authority, you've got two choices: Are you going to seek power to build your own self-image or are you going to empower others, inspiring them to excellence? How you answer will define your success as a leader.

HEAVENLY FATHER, *how can it be that surrendering brings us power and giving away all we have gains us everything? Your example makes that clear. Your example gives me something to shoot for. Help me serve with more compassion. Help me lead with more wisdom. Help me be a servant leader. Amen.*

Your attitude should be the same as that of Christ Jesus: Who, being in very nature God, did not consider equality with God something to be grasped, but made himself nothing, taking the very nature of a servant, being made in human likeness. And ... he humbled himself and became obedient to death— even death on a cross! Therefore God exalted him to the highest place and gave him the name that is above every name, that at the name of Jesus every knee should bow, in heaven and on earth and under the earth, and every tongue confess that Jesus Christ is Lord, to the glory of God the Father.

—Philippians 2:5–11

Day 34: Get Out of the Boat

I've read the last page of the Bible.
It's going to turn out all right.
—Billy Graham

DURING THE LATE nineteenth century, a tightrope walker drew cheers from an appreciative crowd by repeatedly crossing over Niagara Falls on a rope. He asked the gathering, "Now, do you believe I can push a wheelbarrow across and back?" They cheered louder and he made that trip without hesitation. Then he asked, "Now, do you believe I can push this wheelbarrow across and back with someone riding inside?" They cheered wildly. He yelled over the roar, "Who will volunteer?" The crowd became very quiet.

That's a pretty good illustration of the difference between belief and faith. The crowd believed he could do it. Intellectually, they were right with him. But they didn't have enough faith to trust him with their lives. Some theologians explain the difference by saying, "When your belief drops eighteen inches from your head to your heart it finally becomes faith." The Bible tells us, "For it is with your heart that you believe and are justified" (Rom. 10:10).

That's not to say that faith is based on emotions. It's more than that. Faith is knowledge plus an intellectual agreement plus trust—all under the umbrella of love and surrender.

Still don't get it? A vivid scene from the life of Christ will help. On the evening of a particularly difficult day, Jesus sees the disciples out on a boat in the middle of the windswept Sea of Galilee and he begins to walk out to them.

When the disciples saw him walking on the lake, they were terrified. "It's a ghost," they said, and cried out in fear. But Jesus immediately said to them: "Take courage! It is I. Don't be afraid." "Lord, if it's you," Peter replied, "tell me to come to you on the water." "Come," [Jesus] said. Then Peter got down out of the boat, walked on the water and came toward Jesus. (Matt. 14:26–30)

Now, that's faith. How many guys do you know who would set foot on the top of a wave and trust they would not sink? That's an investment of both your head and heart. Peter did pretty well in his shuffle over the waves. That is, until he took his eyes off Jesus.

> *But when he saw the wind, he was afraid and, beginning to sink, cried out, "Lord, save me!" Immediately Jesus reached out his hand and caught him. "You of little faith," he said, "why did you doubt?" (Matt. 14:30–31)*

Even though he had to be rescued, we need to give Peter a lot of credit. He had convictions that should inspire all of us to attempt the impossible. Wouldn't you like to have that kind of confidence? It comes from keeping your eye on the Savior, digging into God's Word, seeing the big picture, and trusting God with every detail of your life.

So are you ready to get out of the boat and really follow Jesus?

HEAVENLY FATHER, *give me a head that believes and a heart filled with a confident faith. I know that when I look to you my confidence grows, but when I look at the circumstances of my life, I begin to doubt. Help me trust you with everything—today and for all eternity. Amen.*

Trust in the LORD with all your heart
and lean not on your own understanding;
in all ways acknowledge him,
and he will make your paths straight.
—Proverbs 3:5–6

Day 35: There's No Place Like Home

When everything is ready, I will come and get you,
so that you will always be with me.
—John 14:3 NLT

JUST ABOUT A CENTURY ago, a missionary couple who had served for a lifetime overseas finally came back to America. As the ocean liner pulled into the New York City harbor, they heard a band and saw a crowd of people cheering and welcoming them with paper streamers. Touched by the show of appreciation, the husband choked back a tear and said to his wife, "Look what the body of believers has done to welcome us home after our years of service." At that moment, the couple saw President Teddy Roosevelt strut down the gangplank, waving to the excited crowd and they immediately realized they had jumped to the wrong conclusion. Soon the crowd dispersed and the husband and wife were left alone on the pier with their tattered steamer trunk and discouraged hearts. After a moment, the husband looked heavenward and stammered, "Lord, we have freely given our lives to your work. Is it too much to ask that a few well-wishers greet us when we return home?" With that, a voice rang out gently from the skies saying, "My child, you're not home yet."

Indeed, authentic Christians need to realize our citizenship is not here on earth. Yes, we can work, pay taxes, make friends, build communities, and strive to make the world a better place. The Bible actually commands us to do all those things. But we are not home. We don't really live here. The Bible says, "Our citizenship is in heaven" (Phil. 3:20).

This realization can go a long way toward helping us set priorities and survive discomfort. For example, if our roofs leak and our bathroom fixtures are the wrong color, it's okay. We've got a mansion waiting in heaven (see John 14:2). If our back aches and our eyesight gets fuzzy, it's okay. Our imperfect bodies will be glorified after our time on earth is done (see 1 John 3:1–3). When we are jealous because the other guy at work got the promotion, our heavenly home address allows us to have an eternal perspective. After all, we're looking forward to a crown of righteousness, which is worth more than any fancy title or corner office (see 2 Tim. 4:8).

Knowing that your home is really in heaven should change your perspective on just about everything you do. And it's a good reminder not to get too comfortable here. If your life is a little too sweet or you're hanging on too tightly to your possessions, you may want to check your address. Your heart and soul have a home on a street paved with gold.

HEAVENLY FATHER, *I can't wait to get home. I suspect you're not finished with me here on earth, and I promise to do your work while I'm here. But I am ready. Even as I work to bring glory to you, I eagerly await the day when I am glorified in your presence. Thank you for heaven. Amen.*

**For, as I have often told you before and now say
again even with tears, many live as enemies of the
cross of Christ. Their destiny is destruction,
their god is their stomach, and their glory is in their
shame. Their mind is on earthly things. But our
citizenship is in heaven. And we eagerly await a
Savior from there, the Lord Jesus Christ, who,
by the power that enables him to bring everything
under his control, will transform our lowly bodies
so that they will be like his glorious body.**
—Philippians 3:18–21

Day 36: Please Fence Me In

Worldly people imagine that the saints must find
it difficult to live with so many restrictions,
but the bondage is with the world, not with the saints.
—Oswald Chambers

THERE'S A POPULAR MYTH that the Christian life is full of rules to follow and boundaries to fence us in. You know what? It's true.

As followers of Jesus Christ, we are saying, "Yes, I acknowledge there are laws that govern the way the world works and the way humans relate to each other." We also pledge, "Yes, I will live within the grasp of Jesus. I covet his guiding hand in my life. I know he has great things in store for me if I stay close to him."

Is that a loss of freedom? Not at all. God's reach is infinite, and therefore our potential is infinite. Those fences that may seem confining to outsiders are wonderfully freeing. They leave us plenty of room to explore our own way, exercise our own free will, and make plenty of mistakes. Plus, living under God's grace means our eternal destiny is secure, and that is the source of unending freedom.

If life has you feeling trapped, stuck in a rut, or not living up to your expectations, God didn't put you in that situation. Very likely, the rut you're in can be traced back to a sin problem. Jesus told his disciples, "I tell you the truth, everyone who sins is a slave to sin" (John 8:34).

Examples of sin that leads to slavery are easy to come up with:

- If you have a habit of lying, you're going to spend a lot of time covering up those lies.
- If you have sex outside of marriage, you're opening the door to all kinds of diseases, unwanted pregnancies, suspicions, worries, and intimacy issues with your future wife.
- If you're envious of your neighbor, you'll spend much of your life chasing things that inevitably

leave you with a stack of credit card debt and an empty heart.

- If you dishonor your parents, family gatherings are destined to be filled with bitterness and ill will.

God's rules exist to protect and provide for us. Go ahead and read the Ten Commandments (see Ex. 20). They are a recipe for fulfilled lives and family contentment. They're all about freedom.

Today, if you or someone you care about is feeling like a slave to sin, don't panic. You don't have to solve the bondage problem yourself. As a matter of fact, you can't do it alone. Only Jesus can. Moments after describing exactly how sin leads to slavery, Jesus explains "If the Son sets you free, you will be free indeed" (John 8:36). That's a promise backed by unlimited power, resources, and love.

HEAVENLY FATHER, *thank you for your laws. Without them, I would probably succumb to my human desires and miss out on many of the joys and opportunities you have waiting for me. Thank you for your protection. Thank you for your provision. Thank you for the freedom you have promised me through Christ. Amen.*

**Then you will know the truth,
and the truth will set you free.**
—John 8:32

Day 37: Knowing God's Will

It is not you that shapes God but God that shapes you.
—Irenaeus

MANY, MANY BOOKS HAVE taken on the challenging topic of "How can I know God's will?" The desire to please God is in itself pleasing to God. It's a question we all need to pose and ponder. But dare we try to solve this mystery in this one small chapter? Let's give it a shot.

First, understand that God's will can be broken down into two categories: (1) God's universal will for all people and (2) God's specific will for each of us as individuals.

Since it pertains to all people everywhere, God's universal will is recorded in the Bible. Sometimes it's very explicit. Sometimes you have to dig. Here are some examples:

- Remember the Sabbath day by keeping it holy (see Ex. 20:8).
- You shall have no other gods before me (see Ex. 20:3).
- Do not be yoked together with unbelievers (see 2 Cor. 6:14).
- Pray continually (see 1 Thess. 5:17).
- Therefore go and make disciples of all nations (see Matt. 28:19).

Those are some pretty explicit instructions: Make church a priority on Sunday. Put God first in your life. Don't marry someone who isn't an authentic Christian. Be in constant communication with God. Share the gospel.

Seeking and obeying God's universal will is a life-long challenge. There are thousands of instructions, guidelines, and commands in the Bible. But there's not a lot of mystery here. God gave us his Word and expects us to follow it. The Bible says it even more clearly: "Do not merely listen to the word.… Do what it says" (James 1:22). His universal will is not just for pastors and Bible scholars. It's "universal."

But what about God's specific will for each one of us? Is he concerned about questions like these: Who should I marry? Which job should I take? Where should I live? What car should I buy? Which tie should I wear? How long should I wear my sideburns? When should I flip the burgers?

Let me confirm that God cares about all of those things. To be certain of the answer to many of these personal questions, you need to go before God in surrendered prayer, seek wise counsel, and follow every instruction of Scripture that applies. But if the Bible is silent about an issue and if your question is specific to you and your situation, please realize you may not get a clear answer from God.

Then what? Make sure you are diligently pursuing God's *universal* will for your life—no small task. Then when you are faced with a decision about God's *specific* will for your life … *do whatever you want to do!* Yes, you read that right. Do whatever will make you happiest! The Psalms say, "Delight yourself in the LORD and he will give you the desires of your heart" (Ps. 37:4).

Men, this amazing freedom to do "whatever you want" is one of God's greatest gifts to you. So don't blow it. Understand that

true happiness comes in service to others. Paul wrote this
warning to all of us:

> *You, my brothers, were called to be free. But do not use*
> *your freedom to indulge the sinful nature; rather, serve*
> *one another in love. (Gal. 5:13)*

HEAVENLY FATHER, *I want to know your will. I want*
to do your will. I want to honor you with every decision of my life.
And give me wisdom, compassion, and courage to make the deci-
sions you want me to make. Amen.

Do not conform any longer to the pattern of this
world, but be transformed by the renewing of your
mind. Then you will be able to test and approve what
God's will is—his good, pleasing and perfect will.
—Romans 12:2

Section 6 · YOU AT YOUR BEST

Day 38: Go with the Flow

No man is an island.
—John Donne

BY NOW YOU HAVE a pretty good idea of how to achieve your best life. You've identified some personal attributes that need a little polishing (or a total overhaul). You're becoming quite handy with your new spiritual toolbox. You've made some life decisions and waded through some pretty deep spiritual concepts. Way to go!

But surprise, surprise. It turns out all that hard work, knowledge, and awareness isn't just for your own benefit. The way the Christian life works is that once you're assured of your own salvation, your focus needs to turn outward. All the gifts you've been given—your natural talents and your spiritual gifts—are not meant to be hoarded. Your neighbors, family, friends, work colleagues, and even your enemies should be on the receiving end of those gifts. But the good news is this: The more you give away, the more fulfillment you'll enjoy in your life.

Let us not become weary in doing good, for at the proper time we will reap a harvest if we do not give up. (Gal. 6:9)

In other words, it's time to allow God's love and mercy to flow through you. It's not unlike the lesson learned from studying the two bodies of water connected by the Jordan River in the land Jesus walked. The Sea of Galilee is fed by spring waters and melted snow flowing from the north. At the southern end of this historic lake—the focal point for many of Jesus' messages and miracles—the Jordan River flows out, thereby irrigating acres of productive farmland.

Fifty miles to the south the Jordan runs into the Dead Sea. It's one of the lowest places on Earth—thirteen hundred feet below sea level. Seven times saltier than the ocean, this lake is aptly named for its water that cannot sustain life.

The difference between these two lakes is obvious to any geoscientist. The Dead Sea has no outlet. The life-giving water from the Jordan River flows in and never flows out. The Dead Sea only takes. It never gives.

In the same way, if we want to enjoy the extreme life promised by Jesus, we need to take all he has given to us and pour it into the lives of others with eagerness and consistency. For those whose lives we touch—and even for ourselves—that can be the difference between life and death.

HEAVENLY FATHER, *thank you for filling me with love, grace, mercy, kindness, forgiveness, and generosity. Help me pass on these same gifts to others. I do ask for blessings for myself and my family but mostly so that I can pass your love on to others. Amen.*

**I have come that they may have life,
and may have it to the full.**
—John 10:10

Day 39: Making Angels Cheer

God is not saving the world, it is done.
Our business is to get men and women to realize it.
—Oswald Chambers

THERE ARE QUITE A few reasons to tell other people about what Jesus did on the cross and what he has done in our lives. First, and most important, Jesus commanded it. Most folks call these final words of Christ the Great Commission: "Therefore go and make disciples of all nations, baptizing them in the name of the Father and of the Son and of the Holy Spirit, and teaching them to obey everything I have commanded you" (Matt. 28:19–20).

Second, our new identity requires it. Once we have accepted God's free gift of grace, he speaks through us: "We are therefore Christ's ambassadors, as though God were making his appeal through us" (2 Cor. 5:20).

Third, there are all kinds of beings in heaven rooting for us. We've been given a clear challenge to lead others to repentance in the following verse: "Since we are surrounded by such a great cloud of witnesses, let us throw off everything that hinders and the sin that so easily entangles, and let us run with perseverance the race marked out for us" (Heb. 12:1). Legions of saints and angels are tracking our efforts and keeping score, "rejoicing … over one sinner who repents" (Luke 15:10).

Fourth, it's personally rewarding. You'll experience joy right alongside anyone you lead to Christ. As John says, "The one who plants and the one who harvests celebrate at the same time" (John 4:36 NCV).

Do you get it? Sharing the gospel is a win-win-win-win proposition. But still, it can be a little threatening. How often have you found yourself in a conversation ideal for talking about spiritual things and there's an obvious opening for you to ask just the right question? Suddenly your mouth goes dry. Your mind goes blank. And the opportunity passes. Don't be too tough on yourself. Jesus understands. That's why he said, "Do not worry about what to say or how to say it. At that time you will be given what to say, for it will not be you speaking, but the Spirit of your Father speaking through you" (Matt. 10:19–20).

In other words, it's not you talking anyway so don't worry about blowing it, and also don't gloat when someone does respond to your sincere invitation. Hey, we're all in this together. We're all sinners in need of a Savior. My friend Steve Brown, respected author and Bible teacher for Key Life Network, puts it this way, "I'm just a beggar telling another beggar where I found bread."

HEAVENLY FATHER, *I want to get to heaven and take as many people with me as possible. Help my life and my testimony be attractive to others. Help me trust the Holy Spirit to supply the right words at the right time. Give me an opportunity to tell someone about you in the next twenty-four hours. Amen.*

Preach the Word; be prepared in season and out of season; correct, rebuke and encourage—with great patience and careful instruction.
—2 Timothy 4:2

Day 40: Life without Love Isn't

If I have a faith that can move mountains,
but have not love, I am nothing.
—1 Corinthians 13:2

MEN ESPECIALLY HAVE A hard time with the word "love." When we consider romantic love, we get all hung up somewhere between commitment and lust. We use the word love to describe our varied relationships with our cars, our kids, the NBA, and our favorite breakfast cereal.

Jesus is very explicit about our need to love. The Pharisees tested him with the question, "Which is the greatest commandment in the Law?" Jesus replied, "'Love the Lord your God with all your heart and with all your soul and with all your mind.' This is the first and greatest commandment. And the second is like it: 'Love your neighbor as yourself'" (Matt. 22:35–39).

But there's more. Beyond the requirement to love God, love our neighbors, and even love ourselves, Jesus also says to "love your enemies" (Matt. 5:44). Proverbs tells us "a friend loves at all times" (Prov. 17:17). When we consider God's love—the fact that he sent his Son to pay the price for our sins—it's beyond the scope of our imagination. Still, all these examples of love don't really get us any closer to a much-needed definition of love.

First Corinthians 13 has become known as the "love chapter" of the Bible and contains a fantastic analysis of how love should act. You've undoubtedly seen the words framed, calligraphied, posterized, and/or decoupaged. I'm pretty sure Rita and I received about five variations as wedding gifts.

Love is patient, love is kind. It does not envy, it does not boast, it is not proud. It is not rude, it is not self-seeking, it is not easily angered, it keeps no record of wrongs. Love does not delight in evil but rejoices with the truth. It always protects, always trusts, always hopes, always perseveres. Love never fails. (1 Cor. 13:4–8)

That's a great list. I recommend you use it as a checklist to see if you are loving your wife, fiancée, neighbors, coworkers, friends, family, and even your enemies. Still it's not a definition. The love chapter describes what love does, not really what love is.

The mystery, I believe, is solved in 1 John, one of the last books of the Bible. And since this is the final day of this devotional, it's a fitting place to end our time together. You should read the entire book sometime, but for right now, consider this short excerpt: "We know and rely on the love God has for us. God is love. Whoever lives in love lives in God, and God in him" (1 John 4:16). Did you catch that? God is Love. If you know God, you know love. All love comes from God. I hope this inspires you to dig deeper and love without hesitation.

Now, lest we put God in a box labeled "love" let me offer a few more biblical absolutes about the Creator. God is Truth. God is Justice. God is Life. God is Mercy. God is Righteousness.

While you are enjoying your best life, you may want to spend the next forty days—or forty years—exploring those theological conundrums.

HEAVENLY FATHER, *help me begin every day and every plan with one pure motivation: to love. Help me love you. Love your Word. Love my neighbors. Love my enemies. Love myself. Help me also to remember any breakthrough truths you have revealed to me these last few weeks. I love you. I trust you. Amen.*

For I am convinced that neither death nor life, neither angels nor demons, neither the present nor the future, nor any powers, neither height nor depth, nor anything else in all creation, will be able to separate us from the love of God that is in Christ Jesus our Lord.
—Romans 8:38–39

Additional copies of this and other Honor products
are available wherever good books are sold.

If you have enjoyed this book,
or if it has had an impact on your life,
we would like to hear from you.

Please contact us at:

HONOR BOOKS
Cook Communications Ministries, Dept. 201
4050 Lee Vance View
Colorado Springs, CO 80918
Or visit our Web site:
www.cookministries.com